$1—
Q

WISE WORDS

for the good life

The Good Life Series

IN 1932, at the height of the great Depression, Helen and Scott Nearing moved from their small apartment in New York City to a dilapidated farmhouse in Vermont. For over twenty years, they created fertile, organic gardens, handcrafted stone buildings, and a practice of living sustainably on the land. In 1952, they moved to the Maine coast, where they continued to give practical meaning to the values that are the basis for America's Back to the Land and Simple Living movements.

To continue this vision of "the good life" beyond their own lives, after Scott's death in 1983 and before her own in 1995, Helen arranged for the creation of The Good Life Center, a nonprofit organization based at their homestead Forest Farm, in Harborside, Maine. The Good Life Center was founded between 1995 and 1998 by the Trust for Public Land, a national organization dedicated to conserving land for public benefit and protecting natural and historic resources for future generations. The mission of The Good Life Center is to perpetuate the philosophies and way of life exemplified by two of America's most inspirational practitioners of simple, frugal, and purposeful living.

Building on the Nearing legacy, The Good Life Center supports individual and collective efforts to live sustainably into the future. Guided by the principles of kindness, respect, and compassion in relationships with natural and human communities, The Good Life Center promotes active participation in the advancement of social justice; creative integration of the mind, body, and spirit; and deliberate choice in efforts to live responsibly and harmoniously in an increasingly complicated world.

Volunteers are the foundation of The Good Life Center. Please contact us if you are interested in visiting, or in lending helping hands to various garden, maintenance, and office projects. Financial contributions help keep Forest Farm open, Nearing publications in print, and educational programs reaching outward.

The Good Life Center
Box 11, Harborside, Maine 04642
(207) 326-8211

WISE WORDS

for the good life

Gathered by

Helen Nearing

Chelsea Green Publishing Company

White River Junction, Vermont
Totnes, England

Dedication

Gentle Reader, I commmit my little Booke to thy gentle judgement. If thou maist receive any profit or commoditie thereby, I shalbe glad of it: and if not, yet favourably let it passe from thee to others, whose knowledge and experience is less than thine therein, that they may gather such things as to them are strange, though to thee well knowne before.

—Thomas Hyll, *The Arte of Gardening* 1608

These curiosities would be quite forgot, did not such idle fellows as I am put them down.

—John Aubrey, *Brief Lives* 1690

If I have said anything here to persuade those of my own Order to love an agreeable Exercise and Recreation: and have taught them how to make something of Interest and Pleasure of those little Parentheses of their Lives, which most commonly go for nothing, I shall have gain'd my End, and the Satisfaction I aimed at.

—John Lawrence, *The Clergyman's Recreation* 1714

First published by Schocken Books 1980. First Chelsea Green edition 1999.
Printed in the United States.

02 01 00 99   1 2 3 4 5

Library of Congress Cataloging-in-Publication Data

Wise words for the good life : a homesteader's personal collection /
     gathered by Helen Nearing. — 1st Chelsea Green ed.
          p. cm. — (Good life series)
     Includes index.
     ISBN 1-890132-41-1
     1.   Conduct of life Quotations, maxims, etc. 2. Country life Quotations, maxims, etc. 3. Simplicity Quotations, Maxims, etx. 4. Quotations, English. I. Nearing, Helen. II. Series.
     PN6084.C556W57   1999
     082—dc21   99-29998
                                                       CIP

Woodcuts from 1800 Woodcuts by Thomas Berrick and His School
Copyright 1962 by Dover Publications, Inc.

"Silence" from *Collected Poems* of Marianne Moore.
Copyright 1935 by Marianne Moore.
Renewed 1963 by Marianne Moore and T.S. Eliot.
By permission of Macmillan Publishing Co., Inc., and Faber and Faber Ltd.

Chelsea Green Publishing Company
Post Office Box 428
White River Junction, VT 05001
(800) 639-4099
www.chelseagreen.com

Contents

Foreword *vi*

Introduction *xi*

The Rewards of Country Living   1

Healthy, Wellthy, and Wise   13

The Work Involved   23

Frugality and Economy   33

The Pleasures and Leisures of Country Life   43

Weather and the Seasons   53

Gardening and the Soil   61

May Building Seize Thee   69

Woodlots and Fire-Making   79

Planning and Management   89

Money and True Wealth   97

The Simple Life Need Not Be Poverty   107

Woman's Place in the Home   117

The Male Point of View   129

Hospitality and Visitors   141

Solitude and Contentment   153

The Evening of Life   161

Index   *175*

Foreword to the New Edition of
Wise Words for the Good Life

Like Helen Nearing, I love books. Helen's love for books led her to old bookstores where she climbed rickety ladders to the highest shelves so she could find out what "treasures" might be stashed way up there. For over three decades, this search brought her to rare-book rooms in many libraries both public and private, where the dustiest volumes awaited her arrival—for she would be one of the few to bring them back into the light in order to glean the "wise words" therein.

My love for books has turned me into a librarian. It took three years of courses to become a professional and then land a job as a reference librarian (a.k.a. "information specialist") in the public library in Waterville, Maine. Locating and presenting exactly what students and readers are looking for is deeply satisfying, but perhaps best of all I too love a dusty old book, especially one that is "out of print." Our library holds a fair number of old literary works as well as "how-to" books published fifty to one hundred years ago.

No wonder that the floor-to-ceiling bookshelves in Helen's living room excited me when I visited Forest Farm in 1995. Helen and I had a conversation about Pearl Buck, since I remembered, during a childhood school field trip to the Nearing house, hearing Helen imply that they had been good friends. At that time, I hadn't known that on Pearl Buck's recommendation, her husband John Day agreed to publish *The Maple Sugar Book* and *Living the Good Life*. At last the Nearings had a publisher who believed in their work!

In 1996, the year after Helen died, I visited Forest Farm for a Monday evening lecture program, and again my hands pulled books off the shelves. It crossed my mind that this was a truly special collection, and wouldn't it be wonderful to catalog it? Little did I know that roughly one year from that visit it would be my personal pleasure to wake up in the yurt built behind the garden wall at Forest Farm, splash ice-cold water on my face at the hand pump, and walk barefoot to work in that same library! Several mornings, shortly after sunrise, I paddled out into Penobscot Bay to look for sea creatures. One day it was so calm that I could hear the breath of dolphins hundreds of yards away. I'll never forget the sound.

During the first half of August, 1997, the gorgeous dry weather encouraged me to do as much as possible of the work outside. Helen's wooden chaise overlooking Spirit Cove was a perfect spot to sit with my laptop and a stack of dusted-off books by my side. What a far cry from the Main Street setting of our library in Waterville, where trucks spew diesel particles that filter through the screens, settling on our shelves and computer equipment. Not to mention the noise! The windows must be open to catch any breeze that might cool off the baked interior. Summer is the time to escape any busy inland town, and it was my luck to be away in Harborside at Forest Farm, now established as the Good Life Center to preserve the Nearings' home as an education center.

During my stay of thirteen days, visitors would arrive to browse the shelves. One man who came with his extended family knew of a special poem he hadn't found anywhere other than at Forest Farm. He asked me if I knew of it. "Not yet," was my reply, since the Metaphysics section on the west wall had so far taken all of my time. It was reassuring to witness people appreciating the collection. Even on the sunniest of days, there were visitors who spent at least an hour inside the library.

I have tried to incorporate into the planning and execution of the cataloging project what I believe Helen and Scott would wish for their collection. In keeping with the Good Life Center's mission of education and access to Forest Farm, I hope that someday the catalog of the Nearing collection will be available through the Internet to scholars and interested parties worldwide. Revealing what is held on these shelves will encourage researchers to visit and use the library. Helen's collection on Death and the Afterlife is comparable and perhaps superior to collections in many academic libraries. She must have been a frequent shopper at Samuel Weiser's occult bookstore in New York City, because about one fifth of the three hundred books in the Metaphysics section had Weiser's sticker on the front pastedown. And Scott's collection on Economics and Socialism, spanning most of the twentieth century, is remarkable as well.

Nearly every book I catalogued exhibited some form of "provenance": signatures, bookplates, and annotations. They speak of their original owner as a diary would, letting other readers in on some intimate thoughts and feelings. Helen spoke to me through the notes in her books, some of which are too personal to relate. She annotated all of the books she used in her own research. Every book she acquired as an adult has the date and the place where she lived along with her initials. Sometimes she added SN for Scott. It's hard to say whether more books have Jamaica, Vt. inscribed on the flyleaf or Harborside, Me. If she were at West Palm Beach when she read a book, she noted that also.

Helen frequently commented in the margins on flyleaves and title pages. She sent books to friends and received mail in reply, which she stuffed into a pertinent volume as if it were a file folder. Her books were a huge filing system. All correspondence relating to a book as well as reviews and newspaper articles have been stuffed inside the covers. Not healthy for the binding, and it warps the cover, but the practice speaks loudly of Helen's way. Like a true librarian, she was probably swift to put her finger on information about subjects that interested her. No need to search for the correct vertical file. It's all on the shelf with the corresponding book!

In my thirteen days at the Good Life Center, there were many sacred moments. Many of the books on Theosophy were passed to Helen after the death of her father, Frank Knothe. There are personal notes to her mother in those books that were gifts from Helen. There are also postcards from all over the world from authors or readers, inserted along with photographs and cut-out memorabilia for future treasure hunters to discover. The toughest decision of the summer was whether or not to remove the inserts and send them down to the Nearing archives at the Thoreau Institute in Concord, Massachusetts. The archival practice is to remove original correspondence for preservation in climate-controlled storage rooms, and to make a photocopy to serve as replacement in the book. A lot of trouble, and extra steps in the cataloging process. Helen's spirit practically shouted at me: Don't bother! After a phone call for confirmation from Ellen LaConte, Helen's biographer, it was easier to relax and proceed. I left most of the inserts in place and removed only those significant to more than the book. One example was a letter from Maria Trapp. She hoped the Nearings would sell their Vermont sugar bush to the Trapp family, taking payments over time, and she wanted to come to Harborside for a spring visit while working on her book, *The Story of the Trapp Family Singers*. Because a letter such as this is deemed historically significant, the original was sent to the Thoreau Institute.

Helen as an insatiable collector of quotes. She spent countless hours, pencil in hand, with books of her own or those of libraries, transcribing the words of the "masters" who went before her.

For this book, first published in 1980, she had to select from hundreds of quotations taken down over the years, and group them. Her chosen topics reflect what was most important to her in life: Rewards of Country Living; Healthy, Wealthy, and Wise; The Work Involved; May Building Seize Thee—and most important to Scott: Frugality and Economy; Money and True Wealth.

Choosing the right words to express experiences and feelings can be difficult. Sometimes while trying to say it right, my mind will race through a mental thesaurus created over the years from high school English vocabulary lists and countless books read. Perhaps Helen thought of the wise words of the ages as I often have: "They have said it better than I could!"

In our city library, the literature that would help foster a broad vocabulary is on the top floor, the least visited area. The most popular books now circulating among youth are the series paperbacks (sci-fi, horror, teen love) put out by large publishing houses who cater to what the average American supposedly wants. This is all so contrived and heavily advertised that if teachers didn't assign works of literature, many young people would not choose to read them. It is rare in our library to meet a young person who is honestly interested in poetry or literature. But just last week a ten year old girl came in looking for everything we had on Celia Thaxter. What a surprise!

For Helen and Scott Nearing, books were a part of the daily ritual. They read aloud to each other regularly. It was for readers like this little girl on her quest for Celia Thaxter that Helen collected the choice quotations gathered here for posterity in *Wise Words for the Good Life*.

In Helen's 1980 Introduction to *Wise Words,* she mourns the advent of microfilm, the format widely used by libraries nowadays to preserve the texts of old newspapers, magazines, and books that otherwise would be destroyed by handling and eventually by burning from the acid in the paper. It is unfortunate that acid was introduced into the paper-making process in order to break down wood pulp, because many books published during the 1930s through the 1970s are browned and pages are falling apart. The Library of Congress is working hard to fund the filming of obscure texts printed on such paper. Fortunately, most of the books in the Nearing collection are printed on high-quality paper, so they will probably last another hundred years.

Helen luxuriated in the experience of reading actual books in the rare-book rooms. She liked the muffled quiet, because she felt that she was "re-entering the womb." Whether she knew it or not, the library at Forest Farm, now the Good Life Center, offers a similar experience. The road to that library is long and winding. One must be determined to travel the distance. Once inside, the lighting is dim around the book shelves unless the sun is shining at a low angle through the west window. And often the stillness is truly palpable, as one may be alone for hours and the stone walls are so thick. Helen and Scott sought and found treasures in libraries and rare-book rooms and used book shops. The Nearing library, built by two passionate seekers, offers similar rewards to those with an open mind.

Thanks to Jen and Jake, the stewards who have called Forest Farm their home for these past two years. They kindly shared their space, and took a sincere interest in the cataloging project, helping me to feel welcome and appreciated.

—*Anne Sheble*
Waterville, Maine
April 1999

Introduction

I love old books. I like to handle them—carefully—enjoying their feel, their bindings, their type face, their paper, their style, and their contents.

I love old bookshops and their accumulated dusty trash and treasures. I frequent them in any village, town, or city where I may be. I have stood on teetery ladders in second-hand bookshops in Bucharest, London, Sydney, and Leningrad; in New York, Chicago, Philadelphia, Vermont, and Maine—ransacking shelves for some out-of-the-ordinary subject or title from organic gardening, to nature cure, to palmistry and astrology, to the Baconian theory on Shakespeare's writings, to death and dying, to homesteading and the good life.

I especially love the rare-book rooms of public or private libraries, where access is difficult without thorough investigation of one's person and purposes. After passing the steely eyes of official custodians, as I ring the bell on well-padlocked doors and am admitted to the muffled quiet of the sanctum sanctorum, I feel as though I am re-entering the womb. The light is dim, the stillness palpable. The privileged visitor sits silently, with only pencil in hand (pens being prohibited, for fear of spots). Talk is only in whispers. Anything louder gets indignant stares from librarians and readers alike. With dangling bunches of keys, hushed attendants flit about, unlocking glass cases and abstracting a book here and there. The atmosphere is positively reverent. One feels privileged beyond most mortals, who are merely reading ordinary books in the public section or, worse, trudging the streets outside.

Here are the memorabilia of ancient times, the archives of great minds, the original editions, manuscripts, and even sacred signatures. Here one is in the company of the great themselves. It is heart-stirring to read their thoughts in such a hallowed atmosphere, and to quote from their works. "Quotations (such as have point and lack triteness) from the great old authors are an act of filial reverence on the part of the quoter, and a blessing to a public grown superficial and external." (Louise Imogen Guiney, in *Scribners Magazine,* January 1911.)

Many days of many years spent reading in rare-book rooms of many libraries have provided me with endless enjoyment and with a large collection of excerpts from choice rare books. During decades of contact with literally thousands of such books, I have been able to dig through material generally untapped and unassembled in the line of my studies. But though my interest is as avid and my ways of research improved through the years, it is increasingly difficult to repeat these occasions of enjoyment and discovery.

Nowadays intimate contacts with original volumes are becoming increasingly difficult. Most of the special books I ask for in libraries can no longer be handled and scrutinized for treasures. Old books must be scanned through a microfilm machine, in an isolated cell. One is given a large inch-wide tape, containing the infinitely reduced type of perhaps four or five books on varied subjects. One must turn knobs, peer as through a microscope, clatter through yards of unintelligible matter of no concern, and when finally reaching the miniaturely reproduced book of one's choice, miss completely the joys of touching and page-turning. No longer can one sit in silent communion with the book itself in hand, and pause, read and reread, looking from page to page.

Few people will again have the opportunity to pore over first editions in the favorable environments I enjoyed in rare-book rooms. Who, separated from the books themselves, can duplicate my rapture in research, and by turning over a page, pounce on some apt term or sentence that exactly illuminates the subject and precisely falls into place? I am lucky to have done my research work when I did, and I am happy to pass on the results of my labors to those who may not have the same freedom of opportunities.

The guiding spirit behind this collection of quotations was a consuming interest in anything well said on the subject of the joys and tribulations of country living. I set out to stalk the sources of sane and simple self-sufficient living, with all its chores and benefits, its defeats and triumphs. The resolve to live life deliberately and purposefully, away from the hustle-bustle of cities, has been touched upon by many authors in many eras. I have endeavored to contact these kindred souls and introduce them to those contemporaries who also are searching for a good life.

—Helen Nearing, 1980

The Rewards of Country Living

When the sun rises, I go to work,
When the sun goes down, I take my rest,
I dig the well from which I drink,
I farm the soil that yields my food,
I share creation. Kings can do no more.

Ancient Chinese 2500 B.C.

Nothing can be more abounding in usefulness or more attractive in appearance than a well-tilled farm. . . . The bank of Mother Earth never protests a draft, but always returns the principal with interest, added at a rate sometimes low, but usually at a high percent.

Cicero, *De Senectute* 45 B.C.

Oh happy (if his happiness he knows)
The country swain, on whom kind heaven bestows
At home all riches that wise Nature needs;
Whom the just earth with easy plenty feeds.

'Tis true, no morning tide of clients come,
And fills the painted channels of his rooms,
Adoring the rich figures, as they pass,
In Tap'stry wrought, or cut in living brass;
Nor is his wool superfluously dyed
With the dear poison of Assyrian pride;
Nor do Arabian perfumes vainly spoil
The native use and sweetness of his oil.

Instead of these, his calm and harmless life
Free from th'alarms of fear, and storms of strife,
Does with substantial blessedness abound,
And the soft wings of peace cover him round.

In easy quiet, a secure retreat,
A harmless life that knows not how to cheat,
With home-bred plenty, the rich owner bless,
And rural pleasures crown his happiness.

Unvex'd with quarrels, undisturb'd with noise,
The country king his peaceful realm enjoys.

Virgil, *Georgics* 29 B.C.

The Country is both the Philosopher's Garden and his Library. It is his Food, as well as Study, and gives him Life as well as Learning. A Sweet and Natural Retreat from Noise and Talk, and allows opportunity for Reflection, and gives the best Subjects for it.

Horace, *Epistles* 20 B.C.

The countrey-man hath a provident and gainfull familie, not one whose necessities must be alwaies furnished out of the shop, nor their table out of the market. His provision is alwaies out of his own store, and agreeable with the season of the yeare.

Don Antonio de Guevara, *The Praise & Happinesse of the Countrie-Life* 1539

The things for to attain the happy life be these, I find:
The riches left, all got with pain; the fruitful ground, the quiet mind;
The equal friend; no grudge nor strife;
No charge or rule or governance; without disease the healthful life.

Henry Howard, Earl of Surrey, *The Happy Life* 1540

The ayre can not be to clene and pure: consyderynge it doth compasse us rounde aboute, and we do receyve it unto us. We can not be without it, for we lyve by it as the fysshe lyveth by the water. Good ayre, therfore, is to be praysed.

Andrewe Boorde, *A Dyetary of Helth* 1542

And though with gorgeous Gates the building high
With earthly greetings alwayes doe not flow,
Nor feeling garnisht gay with imagrie,
Nor rich attire wee see, nor costly show:
Yet stedfast state and life unskild of guile,
With wealth ynough and Pastures wide at will,

And people strong traind up to paine and toile,
And youth with diet small contented still,
Where Godly zeale and vertues all did dwell,
When Justice last did bid the world farewell.

Barnaby Googe, The Whole Art & Trade of Husbandry 1614

Would not amoungst roses and jasmin dwel,
Rather than all his spirits choak
With exhalations of dirt and smoak?
And all th' uncleannes which does drown
In pestilentiall clowds a populous town?

Abraham Cowley, Chertsea 1666

Of Countrey Folk and Shepherds: their Imployment consists of one simple thing, not pestered with many visitors, nor the Impertinent Chat of a Multitude of Customers, nor the Trouble of Bills of Exchange, nor undermining Flatteries of Courtiers, nor litigious Plagues of Mercinary Tongues, or tedious Attendants on Quirking Lawyers, and the like mischievous Encumbrances, which render most Peoples Lives burdensome and divert their Thoughts from all things truly great and Noble; whereas the whole course of their Life is, or may, and ought to be a quiet and delightful study. There is no Occupation more Antient, Honourable or Beneficial, so neither is there any so Innocent and Harmless.

Thomas Tryon, The Country-man's Companion 1684

The infinite conveniences of what a well-stor'd garden and cellar affords. . . . All so near at hand, readily drest, and of so easie digestion as neither to offend the brain, or dull the senses.

John Evelyn, Acetaria 1699

The Blessings of a Country life;
Far from our debtors,
No Dublin letters,
Not seen by our betters.

Jonathan Swift, Letter to Dr. Sheridan 1724

Truly I cannot but here take Occasion to exhort all Philosophic Gentlemen to employ a reasonable Share of their Thoughts and Experiments on the Subject of Agriculture as a more becoming Exercise and Relaxation than Hunting or Cards; and to be sure, more conducing to the Health of the Body, the Strength of the Mind, and to the Capacity of Generosity in the Fortune, than many other fashionable but criminal Excesses. For it ought to be observed that it is an Employment which will at once contract their Wants, and give a larger Ability to supply them; 'twill give greater Relish to the Enjoyments of Life, and make every Part thereof sweetly varied between Ease and delightful Labour. If Gentlemen could persuade themselves to cast their Estates into Beauty and Order, they would quickly experience it the noblest Exercise and greatest Delight.

John Laurence, A New System of Agriculture 1726

A Library, a Garden, A Grove, a purling Stream are the innocent scenes that divert our leisure.

William Byrd, Diary 1740

The more I am acquainted with agricultural affairs, the better I am pleased with them; insomuch, that I can no where find so great satisfaction as in those innocent and useful pursuits. In indulging these feelings, I am led to reflect how much more delightful to an undebauched mind, is the task of making improvements on the earth, than all the vainglory which can be acquired from ravaging it, by the most uninterrupted career of conquests.

George Washington, Letter to Arthur Young December 4, 1788

The country gentleman who resides constantly upon his estate, and endeavours by an attention to the best methods of culture to raise the greatest possible supply for human sustenance, is worthy to be honoured as a public benefactor. While he pastures his flocks and his herds, or ploughs his glebe, he not only affords employment to the peasant, but promotes manufactures, encourages learning, diffuses civility and humanity, and, in general, strengthens the foundations of social life.

Ely Bates, *Rural Philosophy* 1807

I have often thought that if heaven had given me choice of my position and calling, it should have been on a rich spot of earth, well watered, and near a good market for the productions of the garden. No occupation is so delightful to me as the culture of the earth, and no culture comparable to that of the garden. Such a variety of subjects, some one always coming to perfection, the failure of one thing repaired by the success of another, and instead of one harvest a continued one through the year.

Thomas Jefferson, *Letter to Charles E. Peale* 1811

The discoveries in the cultivation of the earth are not confined to the time and country in which they are made, but may be considered as extending to future ages, and intended to meliorate the condition of the whole human race, providing subsistence and enjoyment for generations yet unborn.

Leonard E. Lathrop, *The Farmer's Library* 1826

The benefits experienced by breathing air unconfined by close streets of houses, and uncontaminated by the smoke of chimneys; the cheerful aspect of vegetation; the singing of birds in their season, and the enlivening effect of finding ourselves unpent-up by buildings, and in comparatively unlimited space, are felt by most people.

J. C. Loudon, *The Suburban Gardener* 1838

When I go into my garden with a spade, and dig a bed, I feel such an exhilaration and health that I discover that I have been defrauding myself all this time in letting others do for me what I should have done with my own hands.

The doctrine of the Farm is merely this, that every man ought to stand in primary relations with the work of the world; ought to do it himself, and not suffer the accident of his having a purse in his pocket, or his having been bred to some dishonorable and injurious craft, to sever him from his duties.

Ralph Waldo Emerson, *Man the Reformer* 1841

I shall never rest satisfied till I have three chestnut trees, a potato garden, a cottage, and cornfields at the bottom of some Swiss valley.

Henri Lacordaire, *Conférences* 1842

Would heaven indulge the fond wish of my heart,
I'd ask neither power nor wealth—
With all its allurements of beauty and art,
The world and its grandeur can never impart
The sweets of contentment and health.

In a little cottage, a garden hard by,
And an orchard of fruit-bearing trees;
A site, where no strife or profusion comes nigh.
With a glass of pure water to drink when I'm dry,
I'd enjoy both my freedom and ease.

With books that are useful, selected with taste,
My principal leisure I'd spend;
No part of my time I'd imprudently waste.
On virtue's rich viands I'd mentally feast,
Or converse with a sensible friend.

Benjamin Sharp, in *American Pioneer* June 11, 1842

Would you be strong? Go follow up the plough;
Would you be thoughtful? Study fields and flowers;
Would you be wise? Take on yourself a vow
To go to school in Nature's sunny bowers.
Fly from the city; nothing there can charm—
Seek wisdom, strength, and virtue on a farm.

Anonymous, *Farmer's Everyday Book* 1850

I went to the woods because I wished to live life deliberately, to front only the essential facts of life, and see if I could not learn what it had to teach, and not, when I came to die, discover that I had not lived. I did not wish to live what was not life, living is so dear; nor did I wish to practice resignation, unless it was quite necessary. I wanted to live deep and suck out all the marrow of life, to live so sturdily and spartan-like as to put to rout all that was not life, to cut a broad swath and shave close, to drive life into a corner, and reduce it to its lowest terms, and, if it proved to be mean, why then to get the whole and genuine meanness of it, and publish its meanness to the world; or if it were sublime, to know it by experience, and be able to give a true account of it in my next excursion.

Henry David Thoreau, Walden 1854

I now begin to think myself happy in my present way of life; I cultivate a few vegetables to support me; and the little well over there is a very clear one.

William Shenstone, The Hermit 1868

The density of buildings, the limited area surrounding them, and consequent deprivation of health-giving sunlight, the hum and bustle of the streets and the thousand and one disturbances are all identified with city life. It is an escape from these conditions which makes the restful country such a delight to the citizen.

Edmund S. Morse, Can City Life be Made Endurable?
in Journal of the Polytechnic Institute November 1900

This writer passed his earlier life where the farms were all containing, where we made our own clothing all the way from the sheep's back or the field of flax. We were ambitious in a small way, healthy, patriotic, peaceable, law abiding, and sank upon our pillows with a gentle sigh of comfort and content when we heard the howling blizzard or the rain upon the roof.

We knew nothing of the vaudeville, the passing regiment, the grand opera or the millionaires; but we had ready food and shelter, husking bees, paring bees, raising bees, spelling bees, lyceum lectures, and sleigh rides to the jingling bells through tonic air and over white, spotless creation.

Sometimes we caught a wondering glimpse of the passing creatures of fashion, but we had no covetousness nor envy. Making the morning fire gave us daily energy and appetite; there were no night furnaces to soften the lungs for pneumonia.

We raised produce and traded it at the neighboring store for all the works of art and mechanism we needed. The poorest had what the richest in the city cannot buy—fresh spring water, pure air, fresh vegetables, and above all, limitless scope of action undwarfed by right-angled paths over stone and iron. For the roar of the cities we had the song of birds, the sough of fragrant trees, and that never-ending variety of landscape that the city man loves so well as to pay big money for it upon the painter's easel.

William Hemstreet, *Agrarian Revival*, in *The Arena* February 1903

Those who extol the simple life as the ideal condition of happiness do not mean that want and deprivation of necessities is the ideal condition. The ideal condition is to be found on a farm where the land is paid for and ample means are at hand to supply the necessities for physical demands, with leisure to learn and enjoy those pleasures of the mind which come with knowledge of Nature's laws and wisdom to live in harmony with them, and in a measure comprehend the purposes of creation.

Bolton Hall, *Three Acres and Liberty* 1907

Every duty in the country had a pastime yoked with it. I rose early, not only that I might learn to milk the cows, but that I might see the sunrise; if I went into the woods to saw logs that would presently make a clear flame on the evening fire, my lungs drank health among the forest fragrances; when I worked in the garden I added dainties to my larder.

In the city I lived to work for other people, for my brains were daily exploited that my master might maintain a house at Kensington, and when the landlord, the water-lord, the light-lord, and the rate-collector had all had their dues from me there was little enough left that I could call my own. Here, on the contrary, all that I did had an immediate and direct relation to my own well-being.

W. J. Dawson, *The Quest of the Simple Life* 1907

Do not expect an infinite cure-all in country air and quiet, nor the solution for all Life's problems in hoeing the soil, but learn, by gradual contact with things of the country, that here are benefits no city can give, comforts no modern conveniences can altogether supply.

Richardson Wright, *Truly Rural* 1922

However monotonous it can be, farm work has compensations to be found nowhere else in these times. There is great and fortifying satisfaction in the assurance you can feed yourself and your family. There is good mental and nervous discipline in the tempo of the work, which must be slow if it is to accomplish much. And there is ever the quiet elation that comes only from creative work. One's own products take on new values. Even spinach is highly palatable if you grow it yourself.

Unlike most so-called sports or adult games, farm work for home use is strictly noncompetitive. And while it may not tax the highest reaches of a human wit, still it compels the research of so many of the myriad activities contributing to the maintenance of human life and civilization that it cannot but cultivate the waste places of the mind to a degree nothing else does. To anyone forced to spend eight or ten hours a day in the highly competitive roar and turmoil of the city it is not work at all; it is the finest, most complete relaxation and diversion.

Henry Tetlow, *We Farm for a Hobby and Make It Pay* 1938

Those who are day and night between walls of cement and steel under unhealthy electric light must inevitably become exhausted with words, figures and documents, so that they turn into irritable, quarrelsome, greedy and warlike beings. They estrange themselves from nature. So, if any universal rule could be set up, I wish it might be one to compel every human being, particularly businessmen, industrialists, deadly-minded materialists and pig-headed statesmen and politicians, to come out of their cells and spend a little time with nature each day. Perhaps then—only then—peace would enter all ordinary homes, towns and cities.

Chiang Yea, *The Silent Traveller in New York* 1950

Healthy, Wellthy, and Wise

Now learn what and how great are the blessings that simple living brings in its train. First of all, good health.

Horace, *Satires* 30 B.C.

Good dyet is a perfect way of curing:
And worthy much regard and health assuring.
A King that cannot rule him in his dyet,
Will hardly rule his Realme in peace and quiet.

Anonymous, *Regimen Sanitatis Salernitanum* 11th century

Cleer eir and walking make good digestioun.

Anonymous, *A Diatorie* 1430

Without health all men are poor.

Anonymous, *Proverbs for Daily Living* undated

Those that live in the country are much more healthfull, and are not subject to so many diseases as citizens and courtiers, for in cities the buildings are high, the lanes narrow and durtie, the aire dull and for want of rarification and motion breeds many diseases. But in the country the villages are built at a great distance, the inhabitants are more carefull of their healths, the aire is quick and fresh, the sun unclouded and cheerfull, the earth lesse subject to vapours and noysome exhalations.

Don Antonio de Guevara, *The Praise & Happinesse of the Countrie-Life* 1539

There is no man nor woman the which have any respect to them selfe that can be a better Phesycion for theyr owne saveguarde than theyr owne selfe can be, to consyder what thynge the whiche doth them good, and to refrayne from suche thynges that doth them hurte or harm.

Andrewe Boorde, *A Dyetary of Helth* 1542

Unhappye are they whyche have more appetite than theyr stomake.

Sir Thomas Elyot, *The Bankette of Sapience* 1545

Some seeke for welth, I seeke my helth.

Thomas Tusser, *Five Hundreth Pointes of Good Husbandrie* 1557

Men dig their Graves with their own Teeth and die more by those fatal instruments than the Weapons of their Enemies.

Thomas Moffett, *Helth's Improvement* 1590

Let men take heed how they eate, either of wantonesse, or of appetite. . . . Declare unto mee a dayly dyet, whereby I may live in health, and not trouble my selfe in Physicke.

William Vaughan, *Naturall & Artificial Directions for Health* 1602

Go, tell them what thou bringst exceeds the wealth
Of al these Countries, for thou bringst them health.

John Helme, *The Englishman's Doctor* 1608

If you shall weigh with yourselfe your Estate and manner of living, you will easily confesse with me and lay the blame upon your selfe for such mischiefes. I do not direct my speech only to those who are already affected with sicknes, but to them rather which yet injoy their good and perfect health, to the end they may serve themselves with meanes proper to maintaine the same. For how pretious and deare a treasure it is to be of good health.

John Ghesel, *The Rule of Health* 1631

Nor does this happy place onely dispense
Such various pleasures to the sense;
Here health it self does live,
That salt of life which does to all a relish give,

Its standing pleasure, and intrinsick wealth,
The bodies virtu, and the souls good fortune, health.

Abraham Cowley, *Chertsea* 1666

If we look into the Country, where the Peasant, that has no better than course Bread, and other hard and mean fare, is healthier, stronger, and more agile and sprightful than the City-Cormorant, whose brutish Appetite cannot be satisfied with any other thing than the costliest and richest Varieties that Nature can afford: These latter sort of People accustoming themselves to the highest and finest preparations of Food and Cordial Drinks, are certainly the most unhealthful Men in the World.

Thomas Tryon, *The Way to Health, Long Life & Happiness* 1683

'Tis undeniably one of the most important Businesses of this Life to preserve our selves in Health. But there is scarce one Man or Woman of a thousand that does in earnest consider and pursue the means of preserving their Health, but either lives at Random, or at least takes up with the pernicious Notions of Custom, Tradition and Blind Guides, whose Prescriptions of Diet are most improper and prejudicial, their Medicines Nauseates to Nature, and their Physick a close Confederate with the invading Disease.

Change of Food, Exercises and Airs do work wonders, especially when People betake themselves to more simple Meats and Drinke that are easier of Concoction, and generate a finer and firmer Substance. For if the Food, Drinks, Air and Exercises be innocent and natural, then good Blood is generated whence proceed pure fine Spirits, and consequently the whole Disposition is airy, brisk and pleasant.

Thomas Tryon, *The Good House-wife Made a Doctor* 1692

Were it in my Power, I would recall the World, if not altogether to their Pristine Diet, yet to a much more wholsome and temperate than is now in Fashion.

John Evelyn, *Acetaria* 1699

If People were sensible of what great Importance an intire Simple Life of Order, Sobriety and Temperance is, they would not dare to run such Hazards to humour a liquorish Palate, or rather a debauched Palate, as they do; intailing on their Posterity a Thousand Evils.

What a brave, Serene, Quiet, Delightfull World would there be, if Man would but turn the Eye of his Mind inwardly, and Search, Feel, Taste, See, Hear, Know and Find himself; for when such an one tastes any particular Food or other thing he can distinguish whether it be good and proper to be eaten, how prepared, mixed and compounded, or simple, and what are the Qualifications of it, distinguishing by the Taste for what it is good, and the contrary, and so be able to Embrace the Good and withstand the Evil.

Thomas Tryon, *Letters* 1700

It is most certain that 'tis easier to preserve Health than to recover it, and to prevent Diseases than to cure them.

Dr. George Cheyne, *An Essay of Health and Long Life* 1725

Do we find those who keep great Tables, and live deliciously, healthier and live longer than others? Nay, rather do not those who content themselves with plain Foods, and season them no farther than is requisite for the Health, do better in these Respects than the others.

Dr. M. L. Lemery, *A Treatise of all Sorts of Foods* 1745

Thus still contented with our little wealth,
We eat our wholesome food,—and all the while
Fast by the table stands attendant Health;
And Peace with Temperance look on and smile.

Anonymous, *Domestic Poems* 1773

Preserve a good constitution of body and mind. To this a spare diet contributes much. Have wholesome, but no costly food.

William Penn, *Fruits of Solitude* 1792

It is in a spirited and flourishing husbandry that the soundest health and comfort of nations is found. It is a plenty of food and clothing that are plain and good, rather than fine things, which gives content and cheerfulness to a people.

John B. Bordley, *Essays and Notes on Husbandry & Rural Affairs* 1799

For the bare purpose of preserving ourselves in good health, there needs no better physic than a temperate and regular life.

Louis Cornaro, *The Immortal Mentor* 1810

A very spare and simple diet has commonly been recommended as most conducive to Health. Aim at the happy mean—be Liberal without being Lavish, be Prudent without being Penurious. Plenty of Good Food, plainly but properly prepared, is a Feast for an Emperor.

Dr. William Kitchiner, *The Housekeeper's Ledger* 1825

He who would live on small means must avoid unnecessary calls upon physicians, and the use of unnecessary medicine. Prevention, in a word, instead of cure, should be the motto of him who would live on small means.

William A. Alcott, *Ways of Living on Small Means* 1837

Fly the rank city, shun its turbid air.
While yet you breathe, away; the rural wild
Invite, the mountains call you, and the vales;
The woods, the streams, and each ambrosial breeze
That fans the ever undulating sky—
A kindly sky! whose fostering power regales
Man, beast, and all the vegetable reign. . . .

Here spread your gardens wide; and let the cool,
The moist relaxing vegetable store
Prevail in each repast.

John Armstrong, *The Art of Preserving Health* 1838

I learned from my two year's experiment that it would cost incredibly little trouble to obtain one's necessary food, even in this latitude; that many a man may use as simple a diet as the animals, and yet retain health and strength.

Henry David Thoreau, Walden 1854

We must check our speed. We bring up our children too fast, we work too fast, we dissipate too fast, we eat too fast, live too fast, and, consequently, always ahead of our time, we die too fast.

Anonymous, How to Keep Well, in Harper's Monthly December 1856

It is a notorious fact that while the number of physicians and the expenditure for drugs and medicines is constantly increasing, in every civilized country where they have been much employed, diseases have multiplied in proportion.

William A. Alcott, Forty Years in the Wilderness of Pills & Powders 1859

Many have inquired of me, "What course shall I take best to preserve my health?" My answer is: cease to transgress the laws of your being; cease to gratify a depraved appetite, eat simple foods, dress healthfully, which will require modest simplicity, work healthfully, and you will not be sick.

Ellen G. White, Health Reformer 1866

I have been asked sometimes how I could perform so large an amount of work with apparently so little diminution of strength. I attribute my power of endurance to a long-formed habit of observing, every day of my life, the simple laws of health, and none more than the laws of eating. It ceases any longer to be a matter of self-denial. It is almost like an instinct. . . . I have made eating with regularity and with a reference to what I have to do, a habit so long that it ceases any longer to be a subject of thought. It almost takes care of itself. I attribute much of my ability to endure work to good habits of eating, constant attention to the laws of sleep, physical exercise, and cheerfulness.

Solon Robinson, *Facts for Farmers* 1869

Many are suffering, and many are going into the grave, because of the indulgence of appetite. They eat what suits their perverted taste, thus weakening the digestive organs and injuring their power to assimilate the food that is to sustain life. This brings on acute disease, and too often death follows. The delicate organism of the body is worn out by the suicidal practices of those who ought to know better.

Ellen G. White, *Testimonies* 1900

Sedentary life, rich and sophisticated food, laziness, and comfortable chairs conduce to a slackness of the large bowel, with manifold troubles as a result. The microbes seize on the stagnant food and manufacture poisons which are absorbed into the bloodstream and upset the whole system. To such poisoning (toxemia) half the ills of modern life have been attributed. The promotion of activity of the large bowel will save many a doctor's bill. The soundest way in which to do this is by natural and not by chemical means, or drugs. Foods containing roughage—oatmeal, green vegetables, salads, wholemeal bread, and fruits, especially dried fruits such as figs, dates and prunes—will give the large bowel the stimulus it needs from within, and exercise will give it from without.

V. H. Mottram, *Food and the Family* 1925

Happiness for me is largely a matter of digestion. I have to take cover under an American college president to insure my reputation and respectability when I say that happiness is largely a matter of the movement of the bowels. The American college president in question used to say with great wisdom in his address to each class of freshmen, "There are only two things I want you to keep in mind: read the Bible and keep your bowels open." What a wise, genial old soul he was to have said that! If one's bowels move, one is happy, and if they don't move, one is unhappy. That is all there is to it.

Lin Yutang, *The Importance of Living* 1938

There is something in the freshness of food, especially vegetable food—some form of energy perhaps; it may be certain rays of light or electrical property—which gives to it a health-promoting influence. Certain it is that no synthetic diet that I have been able to devise has equalled in health-sustaining qualities one composed of the fresh foodstuffs as nature provides them.

Sir Robert McCarrison, *Nutrition and National Health* 1944

We are rarely ill, and if we are, we go off somewhere and eat grass until we feel better.

Paul Gallico, *The Silent Miaow* 1964

Wholesome food and drink are cheaper than doctors and hospitals.

Dr. Carl C. Wahl, *Essential Health Knowledge* 1966

The Work Involved

The prudent husbandman is found
In mutual duties, striving with his ground,
And half the year the care of that does take
That half the year grateful return does make.
Each fertile month does some new gifts present,
And with new work his industry content. . . .
So ply your hoes and give the weeds no peace.

Virgil, *Georgics* 29 B.C.

In Maie get a weede hooke, a crotch and a glove,
And weed out such weedes as the corne doth not love.
Slack never thy weeding, for dearth nor for cheape,
The corne shall reward it er ever ye reape.

Thomas Tusser, *Five Hundreth Points of Good Husbandrie* 1557

It hath pleased God to place thee upon a barren and hard soyle, whose bread must evermore be grounded with sweat and labour, that thou mayest nobly and victoriously boast the conquest of the Earth, having conquered Nature by altering Nature, and yet made Nature better than shee was before.

Gervase Markham, *Markham's Farwell to Husbandry* 1620

It must be confessed that the work is great in these beginnings; the men are the horses and oxen, they carry or drag wood, trees or stones. . . . We must look after the cattle, the little ground we have must be tilled, the harvest must be cut and gathered in. We must prepare firewood, which we have to get at some distance away and without a cart.

Paul le Jeune, *Rélation de ce qui s'est passé en la Nouvelle France* 1634

I see no virtues where I smell no sweat.

Francis Quarles, *Enchiridion* 1640

If a garden soile be not cleare of weedes, and namely of grasse, the herbes shall never thrive: for how should good hearbs prosper when evil weeds wax so faste. . . . You shall finde that clean keeping doth not only avoid danger of gathering weedes, but also is a speciall ornament, and leaves more plentifull sap for your tender hearbes.

William Lawson, *A New Orchard and Garden* 1648

The Gardner had not need be an idle or lazie lubber, for so your Orchard will not prosper. There will ever be something to doe. Weeds are alwaies growing.

William Lawson, *The Country House-wife's Garden* 1653

We dare boldly pronounce it: there is not amongst Men a more laborious life than is that of a good Gard'ners; but a labour full of tranquillity and satisfaction, Natural and Instructive, and such as contributes to Piety and Contemplation, Experience, Health and Longaevity.

John Evelyn, *The Gard'ner's Almanac* 1670

Labour and Abstinence are two of the best Physicians in the World.

Thomas Tryon, *The Country-man's Companion* 1684

A Peasant by fasting longer, or working more laboriously than at other times, can thereby heighten the rellish of his dish beyond all the art in the Emperor's kitchin, or Apothecaries shop.

Sir George Mackenzie, *A Moral Essay,*
preferring Solitude to Publick Employment 1685

I think any Man diligently plying himself to Labour seven or eight Hours a Day, may acquire as much as is necessary for his Subsistence. And others in the hardest Circumstances need not labour above ten hours, which is no hard Matter; the remaining fourteen hours being sufficient to Refresh themselves by Sleep and otherways.

James Donaldson, *The Undoubted Art of Thriving* 1700

Love labour: for if thou dost not want it for food, thou mayst for physic. It is wholesome for thy body, and good for thy mind. It prevents the fruits of idleness, which many times comes of nothing to do, and leads too many to do what is worse than nothing.

William Penn, *Some Fruits of Solitude* 1726

The exercise of the Body prevents the Blood and Juices from stagnating and growing corrupt; and the Labourer is every Moment drawing in with his Breath a wholesome and enlivening Stream from the Earth, which causes the Blood and spirits to circulate briskly. Besides, Labour sets an Edge to the Appetite, gives a more grateful and delicious Relish to the Products of the Earth, and at Night disposes the whole bodily Frame into a Capacity for the full Enjoyment of those refreshing Slumbers, that balmy Sleep, which generally forsakes the Downy Couches of the inactive indolent Great.

Philip Miller, *The Gardeners Dictionary* 1731

It is well known that at this Day there are no small Endeavours used to People the waste Places of the Wilderness. . . . Idleness and Sloth in new Plantations are as improper as the Gaiety, Splendor and Luxury of a King's Court would be in a Hermit's Cell. You can turn your Eyes no way in such Plantations, but you will find Invitations and Arguments to Diligence and Industry.

Anonymous, *A Word of Advice to Such as are Settling New Plantations* 1739

What a care, what an assiduity does this life require! A particular friend of mine who possesses a large farm and mows every year about 120 acres of meadow, and keeps 100 head of horned cattle, sheep and horses in proportion, came the other day to dine with me. "How happily, how peaceably you live here," he said. "Your farm is not so large as mine and yet brings you all you want. You have time to rest and to think. For my part, I am weary. I must be in the fields with the hired men; nothing is done except I am there. I must not find fault with them or else they will quit me and give me a bad name. I am but the first slave on my farm." Nor is his case uncommon; it is that of every person who tills the earth upon a large scale.

Michel Guillaume Crèvecoeur, *Letters from an American Farmer* 1782

Unless a gentleman reduces his business to very great simplicity, he will find too great a fatigue, and too constant an assiduity, requisite to render farming of considerable profit.

Arthur Young, *Rural Economy* 1792

It requires ten times more of labor, of vigilance, of attention, of skill, and, let me add, of good fortune also, to carry on the business of a farmer with success than what belongs to any other trade.

Edmund Burke, *Thoughts and Details on Scarcity* 1795

Much has been said of the roughness of the New England soil and climate, and much more than ever was true. Some of our land *is* hard to work, because it wants a more thorough cultivation; and some abounds with rocks, that we may find there the best materials for our dwellings. What is there wanting, then, to make of New England a vast garden? Nothing but contented labour, and intelligence to direct it—and that we have. Let all awaken, then, and try to improve, to the best advantage, the natural abilities of the country—and we shall find that, far from any cause of discouragement, we are greatly favoured.

Thomas G. Fessenden, *The New American Gardener* 1828

If a person is industrious, and so fortunate as to have a family capable of joining in his labours, and living in the bonds of affection, there can be no doubt that he will prosper.

James Pickering, *Inquiries of an Emigrant* 1832

Toil, and be strong. By toil the flaccid nerves grow firm, and gain a more compacted tone.

J. Armstrong, *The Art of Preserving Health* 1838

Hard and steady and engrossing labor with the hands, especially out of doors, is invaluable to the literary man and serves him directly.

Henry David Thoreau, *Journal* November 20, 1851

All my visitors from the city were surprised to see the garden so free from weeds, while they did not fail to notice that most of the vegetables were extremely thrifty. They did not know that in gardens where the weeds thrive undisturbed, the vegetables never do. As to the neighbors, they came in occasionally to see what the women were doing, but shook their heads when they saw they were merely hoeing up weeds. They said that weeds did no harm, and they might as well attempt to kill all the flies. They had been brought up among weeds, knew all about them, and it was no use trying to get rid of them.

Isaac Phillips Roberts, *Ten Acres Enough* 1864

You must be to the best of your strength usefully employed during the greater part of the day, so that you may be able at the end of it to say, as proudly as any peasant, that you have not eaten the bread of idleness.

John Ruskin, *Sesame and Lilies* 1870

The farmer's office is precise and important. . . . He represents the necessities. . . . He bends to the order of the seasons, the weather, the soils and crop, as the sails of a ship bend to the wind. He represents continuous hard labor, year in, year out, and small gains.

Ralph Waldo Emerson, *Farming*, in *Society and Solitude* 1870

Many a farm of ample acreage is left to the rheumatic labor of advancing decrepitude. There is no strength for repairs, no ambition for improvement, and no expectation of more than a bare subsistence. It only requires courage, a cold shoulder to croakers, energy, skill and application.

Commissioner of Agriculture, *Farming in New England* 1871

The same amount of muscular exertion which a town youth puts forth to chase a ball round a twenty acre field would, if properly applied, put a roof over his head and food on his table. The sports of the civilized man are means of life to the natural man. If a man must needs sweat, and be bemired, and have an aching back, it is surely better economy to have a house and a good meal at the end of it all than merely a good appetite for a meal that he has yet to pay for.

W. J. Dawson, *The Quest of the Simple Life* 1907

What is the good life if its chief element, and that which must always be its chief element, is odious? No, the only true economy is to arrange so that your daily labour shall be itself a joy.

Edward Carpenter, *Non-Governmental Society* 1911

I did not set out to dig when I shook the dust of the city from off my feet. Digging was not what my hand yearned for. Some are born to dig; others have digging thrust upon them. I am one of the latter. . . . I wanted to rear calves, and pigs, and poultry, rather than to dig. I wanted, above all, to surround my cottage with a gorgeous orchard planted by my own hands. The quicker, rhythmic movements of manual labour appeal to me more than either digging or hoeing: such as sowing seed broadcast, swinging a scythe in the lush grass, reaping with a hook, or pitching hay into a wagon. Hoeing never fascinated me any more than digging, and I had at first to severely discipline myself to the monotonous stroke of the hoe upon the stony ground.

E. F. Green, *A Few Acres and a Cottage* 1911

. . . Such Gardens are not made
By singing:—"Oh, how beautiful!" and sitting in the shade.

Rudyard Kipling, *The Glory of the Garden* 1911

The chance of success is greatly increased if any members of your household are country bred. A bachelor should seek a wife in the country, selecting a buxom wench, well-broken-in to hard work.

F. D. Smith and B. Wilcox, *Back to the Country* 1942

Coolidge's father was store-keeper and farmer. His general farm, if you like, was a kind of insurance on which he paid a fairly stiff annual premium in vigilance and hard work.

E. T. Booth, *Country Life in America* 1947

A farmer's life may have been ruled by the seasons of the year, but it was not ruled by the clock like a city dweller's. There were no hard and fast hours. At certain seasons one worked 18 hours a day, and at others one worked according to one's own estimate of the necessity.

A. G. Street, *Farmer's Glory* 1951

An old Negro of Georgia, asked what time he went to work in the morning, replied, "Ah doan go to work in the mawnin'. Ah's surrounded with it when Ah git up."

Frugality and Economy

After thy faculty make thyne expences, leste thou spende in shorte space that thynge that thou shouldest lyve by longe. This texte toucheth every manne, from the hyest degree to the loweste.

Anonymous, *The Boke of Husbandry* undated

No man shall ever be poor that goes to himself for what he wants; and that is the readiest way to riches. Nature indeed will have her due, but yet whatsoever is beyond necessity is superfluous and not necessary. It is not her business to gratify the palate, but to satisfy a craving stomach. Bread, when a man is hungry, does his work, let it be never so coarse, and water when he is a-dry. Let his thirst be quenched, and nature is satisfied, no matter whence it comes, or whether he drinks in gold, silver, or in the hollow of his hand.

Seneca, *Of a Happy Life* A.D. 54

Ill husbandry eateth himself out of door:
Good husbandry meateth his friend and the poor.
Ill husbandry taketh; and spendeth up all:
Good husbandry maketh good shift with a small.
Ill husbandry never hath wealth to keep touch:
Good husbandry ever hath penny in pouch.

Housekeeping and husbandry, if it be good,
Must love one another like cousinnes in blood.
The wife too must husband as well as the man,
Or farewel thy husbandry do what thou can.

Ill huswifery one thing or other must crave:
Good huswifery nothing but needfull will have.
Ill huswiferie wanteth with spending too fast:
Good huswiferie scanteth the longer to last.
Ill huswifery craveth in secret to borrow:
Good huswifery saveth today for tomorrow.

The huswife, so named by keeping the house,
Must tend on her profit, as cat on the mouse.

Thomas Tusser, *Five Hundreth Pointes of Good Husbandrie* 1557

In thy heart be truly glad to become a country lad,
Hard to lie, and go full bare, and to feed on hungry fare.

Nicholas Breton, The Passionate Shepherd 1604

Before you come to the New Land, be careful to be strongly instructed what things are fittest to bring with you for your more comfortable passage at sea, as also for your husbandry occasions when you come to the land. For when you are once parted with England you shall meete neither with taverns nor alehouse, nor butchers nor grocers, nor apothecaries shops to helpp what things you need, in the midst of the great ocean, nor when you are come to land, nor yet neither markets nor fayres to buy what you want.

Therefore be sure to furnish yourselves with things fitting to be had before you come; as meale for bread, malt for drinke, woolen and linnen cloath, and leather for shoes, and all manner of carpenters tools, and a good deale of iron and steele to make nails, and lockes, for houses, and furniture for plough and carts, and glasse for windowes, and many other things which were better for you to think of then than to want them here.

Francis Higginson, New England's Plantation 1630

The Acquest of Needless Things tends to the Ruin of the Soul and Body. And, when all's done, the enjoyment of them gives neither Satisfaction to the one nor Health to the other, but makes our Wants the greater.

Thomas Tryon, The Country-man's Companion 1684

Bread and Herbs was sufficiently bless'd with all a frugal Man cou'd need or desire.

John Evelyn, Acetaria 1699

Frugality is good, if liberality be joyn'd with it. The first is leaving off superfluous Expences; the last, bestowing them to the Benefit of others that need. The first without the last begins Covetousness; the last without the first begins Prodigality. Both together make an excellent Temper. Happy the Place where that is found.

William Penn, *Some Fruits of Solitude* 1726

Be always prudent, frugal and cautious in your Expences. There can never be a time when Prudence and Frugality and Caution can be thought more necessary than at such a time. One would think that Persons have abandoned the Conduct of their Reason that will not be prudent and frugal in their Expences at such a Time.

Anonymous, *A Word of Advice to Such as are Settling New Plantations* 1739

Frugality is an enriching virtue: a virtue I never could acquire myself; but I was lucky to find it in a wife, who thereby became a fortune to me.

With frugality, there will be no lack; with extravagance, there's never enough.

Benjamin Franklin, *Poor Richard's Almanac* 1742

A frugal and simple diet, the most coarse and ordinary food is more palatable and agreeable to a sober man's taste and affords him treble the ease and pleasure and advantage than can possibly accrue from the richest and most delicious provision a racked invention can contrive to those of vitiated palate.

L. Lessius, *Health and Long Life* 1749

I would not be understood to recommend a close penurious way of living; on the contrary, I would have every man live well, but live within his income.

Anonymous, *The Way to be Rich and Respectable,* *addressed to Men of Small Fortune* 1780

At this time my farm gave me and my whole family a good living on the produce of it, and left me one year with another one hundred and fifty silver dollars, for I never spent more than ten dollars a year, which was for salt, nails, and the like. Nothing to eat, drink or wear was bought, as my farm provided all.

Anonymous, in *American Museum* 1787

Nothing surely is so disgraceful to society, and to individuals, as unmeaning wastefulness.

Count Rumford *Essay X* 1804

Without frugality few would be rich, and with it, few would be poor.

Ignatus, *Culina Famulatrix Medicinae* 1807

Economy means management and nothing more. The most liberal disposition, a disposition precisely the contrary to that of the miser, is perfectly consistent with economy.

William Cobbett, *Cottage Economy* 1824

Industry must make a purse, and frugality find strings for it.

Esther Copley, *Cottage Comforts* 1825

Even the very humblest classes of society may, and ought to, possess a decent ambition to see themselves surrounded with comforts and conveniences suited to their circumstances, the circle of which they will strive hard to extend by industry and frugality.

A Lady, *The Cook's Complete Guide* 1827

Frugality means the contrary of extravagance. It does not mean stinginess; it does not mean pinching; but it means an abstaining from all unnecessary expenditure and all unnecessary use of goods of any and of every sort. It is a quality of great importance, whether the rank in life be high or low.

William A. Alcott, *The Young Man's Guide* 1834

The true economy of housekeeping is simply the art of gathering up all the fragments, so that nothing be lost. I mean fragments of time as well as materials. Nothing should be thrown away as long as it is possible to make any use of it, however trifling that use may be.

Mrs. Lydia Maria Child, *The American Frugal Housewife* 1835

If a man find in himself any strong bias to poetry, to art, to the contemplative life, drawing him to these things with a devotion incompatible with good husbandry, that man ought to reckon early with himself, and, respecting the compensations of the Universe, ought to ransom himself from the duties of economy by a certain rigor and privation in his habits. For privileges so rare and grand, let him not stint to pay a great tax. Let him be a cenobite, a pauper, and if need be, celibate also. Let him learn to eat his meals standing, and to relish the taste of fair water and black bread. He may leave to others the costly conveniences of housekeeping and large hospitality, and the possession of works of art.

Ralph Waldo Emerson, *Man the Reformer* 1841

Be frugal in that which thou mayest dispense. The hand which in its bounty is guided by folly will soon be left destitute.

A Lady, *The Female Monitor* 1860

Amidst every household toil of a wife, what can be greater than to know how comfort is to be had for the money expended? Chief among the chiefest of evils are wastefulness and unskilfulness in cooking, which cannot be too greatly deplored when there is no money but that arising from a limited income and where there is ignorance of the art of making the most of everything. . . . It is against waste of every kind that one should war. A hospitable heart and economy are twins. We should be careful, that we might be liberal.

Mrs. Eliza Warren, *Comfort for Small Incomes* 1866

Fortunately it is becoming fashionable to economize, and house-keepers are really finding it a pleasant pastime to search out and stop wastes in household expenses, and to exercise the thousand little economies which thoughtful and careful women understand so readily and practise with such grace. Those housewives, especially, whose purses are not over-plethoric, will, we hope, find our pages full of timely and helpful suggestions in their efforts to make the balance of the household ledger appear on the right side, without lessening the excellency of the table or robbing home of any comfort or attraction.

Anonymous, *Buckeye Cookery* 1881

It is a great mistake to suppose that economy consists in buying the poorest articles and in making the table unattractive. The great art is to know where to save and when to spend, and how to use everything to the best possible advantage. There is such a thing as stingy extravagance and wasteful scrimping.

Susan Anna Brown, *Mrs. Gilpin's Frugalities* 1883

I am going to attempt to kill two birds with one stone: to persuade even rich people to insist on a due economy in the consumption of the necessaries of life, and to assure poor people that it is possible to make a good deal more of the scanty materials within their reach than they do at present. . . .

No one will deny the importance of urging rich and poor alike, in the present state of things to try and economise the fuel and food which they may have at their disposal. The sooner we make up our minds that what we regretfully speak of as the "good old times" with their good old prices, will never come again, the sooner we shall cease to look fondly back on a cheaper past, and brace ourselves helpfully and bravely to face the increased cost of the necessaries of life.

Lady Barker, *First Lessons in the Principles of Cooking* 1886

Do not give up in despair because you have a small income, and resign yourself to living meanly, in a hand to mouth fashion. Self-denial and saving and resolute abstention from luxuries will solve the problem.

Mary Hinman Abel, *Practical Sanitary & Economic Cooking
adapted to Persons of Moderate & Small Means* 1890

Let us spare where we may, so that we may spend where we should.

Thomas Fuller, *Wise Words & Quaint Counsels* 1892

The highest compliment, perhaps, that a New England man could give a New England woman: "Thar's one thing I'll say for thet wife o' yourn, Mr. Damon. My hawgs ain't hed a square meal sence she come on the premises."

Bertha Damon, *A Sense of Humus* 1943

The Greeks had just one word for "economize." Our New England grandmothers had twelve: "Eat it up; use it up; make it do, or do without."

Helen Lyon Adamson, *Grandmother's Household Hints* 1963

Almost any woman can cook well if she has plenty to do with. The real test of a cook is to be able to produce a good meal with but little out of which to make it.

Beatrice Vaughan, *The Old Cook's Almanac* 1966

Economy is a poor man's revenue; extravagance a rich man's ruin.

Anonymous, *Proverbs for Daily Living* undated

The Pleasures and Leisures
of Country Life

Let the wealthy and great
Roll in splendor and state
I envy them not I declare it
I eat my own lamb—
My own chickens and ham
I shear my own fleece and I ware it
I have lambs I have bowers
I have fruits I have flowers
The lark is my morning alarmer
So jolly boys now—
Here's God speed the plough
Long life and success to the farmer.

Rhyme on an antique pitcher

A life without festivities is a long road without inns.

Democritus, Ethical Precepts ca. 400 B.C.

Good huswives, whom God hath enriched full enow,
Forget not the feasts, that belong to the plow:
The meaning is only to joy and be glad,
For comfort with labour is fit to be had.

At Christmas we banquet, the rich with the poor,
Who then, but the miser, but openeth his door?
What season then better, of all the whole year,
Thy needy poor neighbour to comfort and cheer.

Each day to be feasted, what husbandry worse,
Each day for to feast is as ill for the purse,
Yet measurely feasting, with neighbours among,
Shall make thee beloved, and live the more long.

Thomas Tusser, Five Hundreth Pointes of Good Husbandrie 1557

As Recreation is most necessary, so to none it is more due than to the Husbandman, and herein you may not expect that I will go about to elect and prescribe what recreation he shall use, binding all men to one pleasure; God forbid: my purpose is meerly contrary, for I know in men's recreations, that Nature taketh to her self an especial Prerogative, and what to one is most pleasant, to another is most offensive; some seeking to satsfie the Mind, some the Body, and some both, in a joynt motion. . . . Never was there any Stoic found so cruel, either to himself or nature, but at some time or other he would unbend his mind, and give it liberty to stray into some more pleasant walks than the myry ways of his own wilful resolutions.

Gervase Markham, *Country Contentments* 1615

Blest be those feasts, with simple plenty crowned, with all the ruddy family around.

Oliver Goldsmith, *The Traveller* 1764

The toils of the day are succeeded by rural amusements, which consist of manly sports, and feats of activity. Away then with pomp and luxury, and leave me in the quiet possession of rural felicity.

Anonymous, *Rural Felicity* 1796

I take it for granted that a farmer ought not to be altogether a man of hard labor, but that his situation should be so far comfortable that the exertions of the body should not preclude that well balanced state of the frame which admits of habitual freedom, and clearness of mind, so that his various operations may be calculated in the best manner to procure the intended results.

J. M. Gourgas, in *The New England Farmer* January 25, 1828

A veritable rural repast ought to take place in the open air, where there should be no other table than the rich verdure of nature; no other seats than the turf, enamelled with flowers; no other shelter than the trees, whose verdant branches ought to be so interwoven as not to deprive you of daylight, but at the same time sufficiently so to protect you from the scorching rays of the sun.

It is then in the midst of a forest or wood, with thickly tufted trees, where a rural feast ought to be held; everything ought to be transported thither in large baskets, which we will suppose is a cold dinner, but which the fire of good wine and your amiable pleasantries will not be long in warming. The zest of your enjoyment and your wit ought to render the dinner exquisite, though even in itself it should not be worth much.

D. Humbergius Secundus, *Tales of the Table, Kitchen and Larder* 1836

Meals are always eaten in-doors, except when, once or twice a year, fantastic folk, wishing to try a short vicissitude and fit of incongruity, choose to share them with ants and earwigs in the open air.

A Lady, *The Lady's Companion* 1851

Picnics have a special enjoyment of their own; and we cannot but regret that with the advance of civilization this good old custom bids fair to be lost, of each one's furnishing a quantum to the entertainment. The opening of the baskets, the droll mistakes, the arranging of provisions, all give birth to hilarity and death to formality. The barriers of society were for the time broken down, and everyone was at his ease.

Have we gained in true real enjoyment by increasing elegance, and requiring no one at present to bring anything but their best dress, their best looks, and their best spirits? We think not, and plead for the good old-fashioned picnic of other days.

Sarah Josepha Hale, *Manners; or Happy Homes &*
Good Society All the Year Around 1868

Let several families living in a city or village unite and leave the occupations which have taxed them physically and mentally, and make an excursion into the country, to the side of a fine lake, or to a nice grove, where the scenery of nature is beautiful. They should provide themselves with plain, hygienic food, the very best fruits and grains, and spread their table under the shade of some trees or under the canopy of heaven. The ride, the exercise, and the scenery will quicken the appetite, and they can enjoy a repast which kings might envy.

Some persons bring upon the campground food that is entirely unsuitable to such occasions, rich cakes and pies, and a variety of dishes that would derange the digestion of a healthy labouring man. Nothing should be taken except the most healthful articles, cooked in a simple manner, free from all spices and grease. I am convinced that none need to make themselves sick preparing for camp meeting if they observe the laws of health in their cooking. If they make no cake or pies, but cook simple graham bread, and depend on fruit, canned or dried, they need not get sick in preparing, and they need not be sick while at the meeting.

Of course, the best is thought none too good for the minister. The people send these things to his table, and invite him to their tables. In this way, ministers are tempted to eat too much, and food that is injurious. Not only is their efficiency at the camp meeting lessened but many become dyspeptics. The minister should decline this well-meant but unwise hospitality, even at the risk of seeming discourteous. And the people should have too much true kindness to press such an alternative upon him. They err when they tempt the minister with unhealthful food.

Ellen G. White, *Counsels on Diet and Foods* 1870

I believe in festival days with all my heart. I think we should sometimes call our friends together, and give them bright thoughts for the intellect, friendliness for the heart, and good things for the palate, keeping as regards the last, within the bounds of common-sense and healthfulness. The palate craves enjoyment; and that craving, being a natural one, must be recognized as such. But what I insist upon is this; namely, that gratifying the palate shall not rank among the chief occupations or the chief enjoyments of life, for it has usurped those positions long enough.

A. M. Diaz, *Papers Found in the School Master's Trunk* 1875

There is no more wholesome or satisfactory method of entertainment— cheap or dear—than an afternoon tea or noon-day lunch in the woods in fine summer weather. If the dwellers in American cottages would expend half the sum per season in this kind of merry-making that goes to the getting-up of a single high tea or evening party served in a crowded room to people who are not hungry, the race would be happier and healthier. A "basket-picnic" served in a grove accessible by a short walk from railway station or street-car terminus needs only a summer sky, chosen friends, and good spirits to make it a social success. Whatever tempts to such holidays for our over-worked, over-anxious men and women, is an experiment in active benevolence we do well to try.

Ask your guests to take shovels and water-proofs. In the driest weather it is never prudent to sit on the ground without such protection. . . . Take care to pitch your sylvan tent in contiguity to well, spring, or brook, from which you can get water for filling up lemonade-jar and water-pail. . . . Arrived at the appointed place, serve your little feast while daylight lasts, postponing strolls, boating, and games until it is over. Make a frolic of setting the table. Young and old will enter zestfully into the business of the hour.

The ladies should be seated alternately with attendants of the other sex, and the waiting, replenishing glasses and plates, etc., be done by the latter. Have a certain easy decorum in the appointment and conduct of the collation, holding the direction of this in your own hands. Impress by your example and bearing what gay young people are prone to forget under the influence of out-door air and scenes, to wit, that informality and lawlessness are not interchangeable terms. Stand as pleasantly upon the order of your feast as you will, but do not let it degenerate into a scramble.

Marion Harland, *The Cottage Kitchen* 1883

As long as the great American picnic-goer likes pickles, you may as well provide them, for the relief of possible bilious tendencies. . . . No, I shall not forget the cake, and you may depend on its being the only thing that other people will not forget either. . . . Twice as many cookies, jumbles, ginger snaps and biscuits will prove almost enough for the most hardened picnic eaters. . . . If you want the older ladies to enjoy the picnic and go home without fatigue and neuralgic twinges, provide all the canvas camp-chairs, mats and pieces of carpets possible to give people easy seats.

What is left at picnics ought not to be wasted in the wholesale manner common. I have seen wagon loads of young people pelting each other with the half-hundred cream cakes left from lunch. Good taste and thrift forbid such monkeyish performances.

Mrs. S. D. Power, *Anna Maria's House-Keeping* 1884

Life, to a large extent, was cooperative in the early days; the people helped one another. It would, indeed, have been very dull in the backwoods and remote country places if it had not been for their frequent social gatherings (their quilting bees, husking bees, barn raisings etc.) where work and play were combined.

A Canuck, *Pen Pictures of Early Pioneer Life in Upper Canada* 1905

If there is one impression I should be distressed to convey, it is that life on a home-use farm is all work and no play. Far, far from it. . . . Much of the farm work itself is a more satisfactory substitute for adult outdoor games.

Henry Tetlow, *We Farm for a Hobby and Make It Pay* 1938

Like a good pioneer, father hankered to eat outdoors. And he ate outdoors, come gale, come zephyr. . . . Outdoors put an edge on my father like that on a new-filed saw. Even mussels seemed worth eating when we ate them out in the wind and the sun. But father didn't rest content with just eating the food he had got together and cooked for himself outdoors. He insisted on eating his regular meals out in the open also. He built mother a cook-house for Summer, and she had to do her cooking out there.

Beyond the cook-house, under the oaks that dipped their eastern leaves in the ocean, father built him a table, with benches all the way around it, and mother had to serve our meals there. The wind blew up the tablecloth. We had to anchor it down with big stones. Things cooled off. The tea went flat and chilled. Ants got into the sugar. Fuzzy caterpillars dropped into our milk. Bees got into the syrup and into father's trousers. Bees stung father. But eat out under the sky he would.

I can see father and all of us out there under the oaks even yet. A dozen of us round one table. Girls with honey-colored hair flowing in the wind, little boys' spiralled curls ruffling up. Golden bumble-bees blazing past. A stiff breeze up. Butterflies lighting on the rim of the milk-pitcher. The sunlight making polka dots on our noses and the tablecloth, as it spilled down through the oak leaves. The whole deep sky blue above us, dappled with fair-weather clouds. . . . Seagulls leaning white on the wind. And father with his big brown moustache all one way in the wind, the wind in his blue eyes, making them twinkle. Father smiling and eating hugely and shouting out between mouthfuls— "Yes, Sir! This is the way to live! Out in the air, out where a man belongs!"

Robert P. Tristram Coffin, *Mainstays of Maine* 1944

Inherent in every adult masculine heart there remains some of the qualities of a small boy. He is secretly plagued by a spirit of pyro-mania and he delights in playing with fires. In common with the small boy, he enjoys food, lots of food, especially when it is prepared and eaten in an atmosphere of cheerful informality out-of-doors.

Esquire's Handbook of Food 1949

Weather and the Seasons

Now welcome, somer, with thy sonne softe,
That hast this wintres wedres overshake.

Geoffrey Chaucer, *The Parliament of Fowls* 1380

The Spring visiteth not these Quarters so timely. Summer imparteth a verie temperate heat, recompencing his slow fostering of the fruits with their kindly ripening. Autumne bringeth a somewhat late harvest. In Winter we cannot say the Frost and Snow come verie seldome and make a speedie departure.

Richard Carew, *The Survey of Cornwall* 1602

I do hold it, in the Royal Ordering of Gardens, there ought to be Gardens for all the Months in the Year.

Sir Francis Bacon, *Sylva Sylvarum* 1605

Summer's lease hath all too short a date.

William Shakespeare, *Sonnet 18* 1609

All Creatures that are born and bred in cold Climates are stronger and better able to endure Hardship and toilsom Labour than those that live in hot Climates. So great is the power and operation of open cold Air it does wonderfully strengthen Nature.

Thomas Tryon, *The Way to Health, Long Life and Happiness* 1691

What ought to be done today, do it; for tomorrow it may rain.

Jared Eliot, *Hints to Farmers* 1760

The cold in winter is less intense, the air in summer purer, and the country in general much more wholesome.

Anonymous, *American Husbandry* 1775

Snow is beneficial to the ground in winter, as it prevents its freezing to so great a depth as it otherwise would. It guards the winter grain and other vegetables, in a considerable degree, from the violence of sudden frosts, and from piercing and drying winds.

The later snow lies on the ground in spring, the more advantage do grasses and other plants receive from it. Where a bank of snow has lain very late, the grass will sprout, and look green earlier, than in parts of the same field which were sooner bare.

In the northern parts of New England the ground in some years is covered with snow for four months, even in the cultivated fields. This is not regretted by the inhabitants as they find it is a great advantage for drawing masts, logs, lumber, and wood upon sleds, which is much easier than carting them. The roads are also far better when the ruts and sloughs are filled, and every part paved with ice, or condensed snow. The winters, tedious as they are, seem too short for the teamsters.

Samuel Deane, The New-England Farmer 1790

> Therefore all seasons shall be sweet to thee,
> Whether the summer clothe the general earth
> With greenness, or the redbreast sit and sing
> Between the tufts of snow on the bare branch.

Samuel Taylor Coleridge, Frost at Midnight 1798

> Observe the circling year: how unperceived
> Her seasons change! behold, by slow degrees,
> Stern winter tamed into a ruder spring,
> The ripened spring a milder summer glows;
> Departing summer sheds Pomona's store;
> And aged autumn brews the winter storm.

Anonymous, The Seasons undated

In March it is time for winter to depart, but he may be compared to a crocodile, who, having paid you a visit and staid as long as he ought, pretends to go away; but while he puts his head and body out of doors, leaves his huge tail writhing, bending and brandishing behind. Thus, during March, winter's tail is left to annoy us with squalls, gusts, tempests, rain, hail, snow. There often seems to be a strife between the seasons, spring and winter alternately getting the ascendancy. But, after a while, the latter finds his icicles melting away, and to avoid being reduced to a stream of water, he slowly retreats, first to New England, lingering along the Green Mountains, till pursued by the Genius of Flowers, he flees across Hudson's Bay and hides himself behind the hills of Greenland till he can venture out again with safety.

Peter Parley's Almanac for 1836

'Tis merry, merry in the spring,
And merry in the summer time,
And merry when the great winds sing
Through autumn's woodlands brown—
And in the winter, wild and cold,
'Tis merry, merry too.

William Howitt, *Good in All Seasons* 1850

They who come to this world as to a watering-place in the summer for coolness and luxury never get the far and fine November views of heaven.

Henry David Thoreau, *Journal* May 9, 1852

I do not quite like this warm weather and bare ground at this season. What is a winter without snow and ice in this latitude? The bare earth is unsightly. This winter is but unburied summer.

Henry David Thoreau, *Journal* January 24, 1858

You say you fear the rigours of the Canadian winter will kill me. I never enjoyed better health, nor so good, as since it commenced. There is a degree of spirit and vigour infused into one's blood by the purity of the air that is quite exhilarating. The very snow seems whiter and more beautiful than it does in our damp vapoury climate.

C. P. Traill, *Backwoods of Canada* 1860

Winter having passed away, the time for labor and the singing of birds again returned. . . . It was now the season for me to bustle about, fix up my land, and get in my crops.

Isaac Phillips Roberts, *Ten Acres Enough* 1864

O suns and skies and clouds of June,
And flowers of June together,
Ye cannot rival for one hour
October's bright blue weather.

Helen Hunt Jackson, *Verses* 1884

Warm summer sun, shine friendly here;
Warm western wind, blow kindly here.

Richard Richardson, *To Annette* 1890

New England has a good climate . . . the finest climate in the world. . . . If we have coarse days, and dog days, and white days, and days that are like ice-blinks, we have also yellow days, and crystal days,— days which are neither hot nor cold, but the perfection of temperature.

Ralph Waldo Emerson, *Country Life* 1893

It is curious how extraordinarily susceptible some of us are to the influences of weather, and even to those of the different seasons. I do not think that these affect the dwellers in town so much, for, their existence being more artificial, the ties which bind them to Nature are loosened, but with folk who live in the country and study it, it is otherwise. Every impulse of the seasons throbs through them, and month by month, even when they are unconscious of it, their minds reflect something of the tone and colour of the pageant of the passing day. After all, why should it not be so, seeing that our bodies are built up of the products of the earth, and that in them are to be found many, if not all, of the elements that go to make the worlds, or at any rate our world, and every fruit and thing it bears. The wonder is not that we are so much in tune with Nature's laws and phases but that we can ever escape or quell their mastery.

H. Rider Haggard, *A Farmer's Year* 1899

I cannot conceive the Spring of lands that have no Winter. I take my Winter gladly, to get Spring as a keen and fresh experience.

The Odd Farmwife, *The Odd Farmhouse* 1913

To me, Spring is a movement, a mighty surging upward. It isn't coaxed from above, but moved from below. The growing things break upward through the crust of chill earth the way a man gets out of bed on a zero morning—gradually, reluctantly, cover by cover, a toe at a time; not because someone has waked him, but because he has accumulated the necessary refreshment of sleep and is ready to go forth and do the day's work.

Richardson Wright, *Truly Rural* 1922

The country, like any Queen, is ever attended by scrupulous lady's-maids in the guise of the seasons, and the town hath but one dress of brick turned up with stone; but the country hath a brave dress for every week in the year; sometimes she changes her dress twenty-four times in twenty-four hours; and the country weareth her sun by day as a diamond on a Queen's brow, and the stars by night as necklasses of gold beads, whereas the town's sun is smoky paste, and no diamond, and the town's stars are pinchbeck and not gold.

Herman Melville, *Pierre* 1929

I do not suppose there was a moment in the waking life of an agricultural labourer when he was unconscious of the weather. He noted instinctively when the wind changed, and considered its possible effect on his life and work and upon those of his neighbors. . . . If, on a wet day, you meet a man who greets you with the remark that it is a nice day, you may rest assured that you have met a true son of the soil, who knows that all sorts of weather are necessary.

A. G. Street, *Farmer's Glory* 1951

One thing I know about March—whether it storms or shines, it is the key to spring. It can be a sun-warmed day, or a wet one, or a cold; but a key just the same.

Faith Baldwin, *Harvest of Hope* 1962

I never remember which is the calendar's first day of spring; but every year one day comes, when, although there is no obvious change in the appearance of trees and hedges, the earth seems to breathe, and it is spring.

Elizabeth Clarke, *The Darkening Green* 1964

Gardening and the Soil

If you would be happy for a week, take a wife; if you would be happy for a month, kill a pig; but if you would be happy all your life, plant a garden.

Ancient Chinese proverb

To be a successful farmer one must first know the nature of the soil.

Xenophon, *Oeconomicus* 400 B.C.

What I enjoy is not the fruits alone, but I also enjoy the soil itself, its nature and its power.

Cicero, *De Senectute* 45 B.C.

Lay durt upon heapes, some profit it reapes.
A rottenly mould is land woorth gould.

Thomas Tusser, *Five Hundreth Pointes of Good Husbandrie* 1557

Experiments touching all Manner of Composts, and Helps of Ground: the Fourth Help of Ground is, the Suffering of Vegetables to dye into the Ground; And so to Fatten it: As the Stubble of Corne, Especially Pease. Brakes cast upon the Ground, in the beginning of Winter, will make it verie Fruitfull. It were good to trie, whether Leaves of Trees swept together, with some Chalke and Dung mixed, to give them more Heart, would not make a good Compost; for there is nothing lost so much as Leaves of Trees.

Sir Francis Bacon, *Sylva Sylvarum* 1605

What can your eye desire to see, your ears to hear, your mouth to take, or your nose to smell that is not to be had in a garden?

William Lawson, *A New Orchard and Garden* 1648

If a man want an Appetite to his Victuals, the smell of the Earth new turned up, by digging with a Spade, will procure it.

William Coles, *The Art of Simpling* 1656

Gardening is one of the best-natured delights of all others, for a man to look about him, and see nothing but the effects and improvements of his own art and diligence; to be always gathering some fruits of it, and at the same time to behold others ripening, and others budding; to see his soil covered with the beauteous creatures of his own industry; and to see, like God, that all his works are good.

Abraham Cowley, *Of Agriculture* 1668

Lay your material in a large heap, in some convenient place: A layer of fresh and natural Earth, taken from the Surface, and another of dung, a pretty deal thicker, then a layer of Earth again, and so successively, mingling a load of lime to every ten loads of dung, will make an admirable Compost, somewhat shaded, so as neither the Sun too much draw from it, nor the violent rains too much dilute it.

John Rose, *The English Vineyard Vindicated* 1675

Have allways ready prepar'd several Composts, mixed with natural pasture earth, a little loamy: skreene the mould, and mingle it discreetly with rotten Cow-dung; not suffering it to abide in heapes too long, but be frequently turning and stirring it, nor let weedes grow on it; and that it may be moist and sweete, and not wash away the salts, it were best kept and prepared in some large pit, or hollow place which has a hard bottom and in the shade.

John Evelyn, *Directions for the Gardiner* 1687

Mr. Masters of Pennsylvania, an ingenious and publick-spirited Farmer, was so good as to write me a letter, to inform me how he increased his Dung; his Way is to hire poor Children to gather up the fallen dry Leaves in the Woods and by Fence Sides; puts them up in Stocks to settle, then carts them home, puts them into his Yards, his Stables and Cow-Houses, where they are poached and trampled in together, with the Dung and Stale of his Cattle; and in the Conclusion, makes a great Increase of Manure; he has tried it so far, and so much, as to know it to be a great Improvement.

Jared Eliot, *Essays upon Field-Husbandry in New-England* 1760

Leaves of trees are useful as a manure, excepting those of the resinous kinds. They should be collected into farm-yards, trampled by cattle, and mixed with their excrements. Some recommend leaves of oak, for hot beds, instead of tanner's bark, as by fermenting more slowly they afford a more regular and permanent heat.

Samuel Deane, *The New-England Farmer* 1790

A compost dung hill appears to him an object of so great importance to the improvement of the land that, of all branches of labour, he regrets the want of assistants in this the most; and waits, as a singular blessing, the time when his children shall be capable of contributing their share: so thoroughly is he persuaded that he wants only labouring hands to procure fifty loads more of manure, without increasing the number of his cattle.

Anonymous, *Massachusetts Agricultural Repository & Journal* 1815

Be very careful not to suffer weeds of any sort to ripen their seeds on or anywhere within gunshot of your mines, or mints, for making money, which your manure-heaps and compost-beds may be styled, almost without a metaphor.

Anonymous in *The New England Farmer* August 21, 1824

The greatest blessings which a kind Providence can bestow on man, in his sublunary state of existence, are: health of body and peace of mind; and the pursuits of gardening eminently conduce to these.

Thomas G. Fessenden, *The New American Gardener* 1828

My yards are constructed on a small loam, resting on a clay subsoil. Here should be annually deposited, as they can be conveniently collected, the weeds, coarse grass, the brakes of the farm; and also the pumpkin vines and potato tops. The quantity of these upon a farm is very great, and are collected and brought to the yard with little trouble by the teams returning from the fields. And here also should be fed out, or strewed as litter, the hay, stalks, and husks of Indian corn, pea and bean haulm, and the straw of grain not wanted in the stables. To still further augment the mass, leached ashes and swamp earth may be added to advantage. These materials will absorb the liquid of the yard, and, becoming incorporated with the excrementitious matter, double or treble the ordinary quantity of manure.

Thomas G. Fessenden, *The Complete Farmer & Rural Economist* 1835

In our present imperfect condition, a beneficent Providence has not reserved a moderate success in Agriculture exclusively to the exercise of a high degree of intelligence. His laws have been so kindly framed, that the hand even of uninstructed toil may receive some requital in remunerating harvests; while their utmost fulness can be anticipated only where corporeal efforts are directed by the highest intelligence.

R. L. Allen, *The American Farm Book* 1849

The leaf harvest is one of importance to the farmer if he will but avail himself of it. A calm day or two spent in this business will enable him to put together a large pile of these fallen leaves. . . . Gardeners prize highly a compost made in part of decomposed leaves. The leaf-harvest is the last harvest of the year, and should be thoroughly attended to at the proper time.

Isaac Phillips Roberts, *Ten Acres Enough* 1864

Who loves a garden still his Eden keeps,
Perennial pleasures plants, and wholesome harvest reaps.

Amos Bronson Alcott, *Tablets* 1868

To own a bit of ground, to scratch it with a hoe, to plant seeds, and watch the renewal of life—this is the commonest delight of the race, the most satisfying thing a man can do.

Charles Dudley Warner, *My Summer in a Garden* 1870

There cannot be a more healthy or pleasing pursuit than gardening, invigorating both to mind and body, and possessed of important educating influences. And as a means of recreation to owners, gardening not only braces the nerves, and imparts a healthful glow to the body, but imparts a thousand pleasing emotions to the inner feelings.

S. O. Beeton, *All About Country Life* 1871

O the green things growing, the green things growing,
The faint sweet smell of the green things growing!

Dinah Mulock Craik, *Poems* 1880

Today two carts are carrying refuse to be scattered on that part of the nine acres which is coming for rest, or on so much of it as we can spare time and horses to cover. We have been at the task for nearly a week, sometimes with two and sometimes with three carts, and I think have spread about fifty loads upon the root land. This compost is the best manure which I have ever used. . . . For a root crop I would rather use it than any expensive artificial dressing on the market.

H. Rider Haggard, *A Farmer's Year* 1899

One hears a lot about the rules of good husbandry; there is only one—leave the land far better than you found it.

George Henderson, *The Farming Ladder* 1944

May Building Seize Thee

It will not always be summer: build barns.

Hesiod, *Works and Days* ca. 800 B.C.

In his early manhood the head of the household should be eager to plant his land. He should think long before building but he should not think about planting, but plant. When you have approached the age of 36 years you should build, if you have your land well planted. Build in such a way that the farm buildings will not find fault with the farm nor the farm with the buildings. . . .

If you are going to contract for the building of a new farmstead from the ground up, the builder should do the following: He should build all the walls, as he is directed, of lime mortar and small stones; he should prepare the supporting pieces of squared stone and all the building timbers that are needed, the thresholds, the doorposts, the lintels, the beams, the supports, and build the winter stable for the work oxen.

Cato the Censor, *De Agricultura* 160 B.C.

Would I a house for happiness erect,
Nature alone should be the architect.
She'd build it more convenient than great,
And doubtless in the country choose her seat.

Horace, *Odes*, Book I 20 B.C.

A man must consider the expense before he do begin to build; for there goeth to building many a nail, many pins, many laths and many tiles or slates or straws beside other great charges, as timber, boards, lime, sand, stones or brick, beside the workmanship and the implements. . . .

Whosoever will build a mansion place or house, he must be sure to have both water and wood. For profit and health of his body, he must dwell at elbow room, having water and wood annexed to his place or house; for if he be destitute of any of the principals, that is to say, first, of water for to wash and wring, wood to bake and brew, it were a great discommodious thing. And better it were to lack wood than water, although that wood is a necessary thing, not only for fuel, but also for other urgent causes, specially concerning building and repairs.

Andrewe Boorde, *The Dyetary of Helth* 1542

No dwellers, what profiteth house for to stand?
What goodness, unoccupied, bringeth the land?

Whoever rears his house in air,
Will need much gold to keep it there;
While he that builds an humble cot
May save some gold to boil the pot.
Who has the cot ne'er wants a home;
Who spent the gold, to want may come.

Thomas Tusser, *Five Hundreth Pointes of Husbandrie* 1557

In times past men were contented to dwell in houses builded of sallow, willow, plum tree, hard-beane, and elme, so that the use of oke was in manner dedicated wholie unto churches, religious houses, princes palaces, noblemen's lodgings, and navigation, but now all these are rejected, and nothing but oke anie whit regarded. And yet see the change, for when our houses were builded of willow, then had we oken men, but now that our houses are come to be made of oke, our men are become willow. . . .

Never so much oke hath been spent in a hundred years before as in ten years of our time, for everie man almost is a builder, and he that hath bought any small parcel of ground, be it ever so little, will not be quiet till he have pulled downe the old house, if anie were there standing, and set up a new after his own device. . . .

In the proceeding of their workes how they set up, how they pull downe, how they enlarge, how they restreine, how they ad to, how they take from, whereby their heads are never idle, their purses never shut, nor their bookes of account never made perfect.

Raphael Holinshed, *The Chronicles of England, Scotlande and Irelande* 1577

For my part, I build my house, as they say, according to my purse, agreeable to my calling, and to my living.

Barnaby Googe, *The Whole Art and Trade of Husbandry* 1614

If the Place wherein he was borne, which he enjoyeth by right of Succession, or Purchase, be not naturally as fit and convenient as that he may thereby be drawne and allured with the love of it; then he must endevour so to fit it by his skill, and endevour by his labour so carefully to amend and correct it, that it may be sufficient for the maintaining of him and those that belong unto him. . . .

Your Lodging or Mansion shall have no more than this one storie, about which you shall raise no other save only your Garners and Galleries, keeping your house thereby of a lower pitch, and so lesse subject to the rage of the Winds, which will save you a great deale of charges, when as you shall not be forced to use the helping hand of Tylers every houre.

Gervase Markham, *The Countrey Farme* 1616

For the building of houses, townes, and fortresses, where shall a man finde the most conveniency, as stones of most sorts.

Captaine John Smith, *Advertisements for the
Unexperienced Planters of New-England or Anywhere* 1631

Take care that it be well water'd and wooded, that it have a good ascent to it, which makes a House wholesome, and gives opportunity for good Cellaridge, and likewise a good Prospect is very pleasant according to the variety it affords.

J. Mortimer, *The Whole Art of Husbandry* 1712

The plenty of timber in this country is a great advantage to new settlers, in rendering their buildings and many of their utensils of no other expence than that of labour, tools, and a little iron.

Anonymous, in *American Husbandry* 1775

The inhabitants of Europe, who dwell in houses of stone or brick, are surely as healthy as those of Virginia. These houses have the advantage, too, of being warmer in winter and cooler in summer than those of wood; of being cheaper in their first construction, where lime, and stone, is convenient, and infinitely more durable.

In Virginia the private buildings are very rarely constructed of stone or brick, much the greatest portion being of scantling and boards, plastered with lime. It is impossible to devise things, more ugly, uncomfortable, and happily more perishable.

Thomas Jefferson, *Notes on Virginia* 1784

The evil in our architecture lies principally in this—that we build of wood. From this custom much immediate as well as remote inconvenience is to be expected. The comfort arising from celerity and dispatch does not make up for the numerous considerations of perishableness, want of safety, and call for repairs. . . . Bachelors only ought to build of wood—men who have but a life estate in this world, and who care little for those who come after them.

Anonymous, in *The American Museum* October 1790

If I were commencing life again in the woods, I would not build anything of logs except a shanty or a pig-sty; for experience has plainly told me that log buildings are the dirtiest, most inconvenient, and the dearest, when everything is taken into consideration. As soon as the settler is ready to build, let him put up a good frame, roughcast, or stone house, if he can possibly raise the means, as stone, timber, and lime cost nothing but the labour of collecting and carrying the materials. When I say that they "cost nothing," I mean that no cash is required for these articles, as they can be prepared by the exertion of the family.

Samuel Strickland, *Twenty-seven Years in Canada West* 1853

Much it concerns a man, forsooth, how a few sticks are slanted over him or under him, and what colors are daubed upon his box. It would signify somewhat, if, in any earnest sense, *he* slanted them and daubed it. . . .

There is some of the same fitness in a man's building his own house that there is in a bird's building its own nest. Who knows but if men constructed their dwelling with their own hands, and provided food for themselves and families simply and honestly enough, the poetic faculty would be universally developed, as birds universally sing when they are so engaged? But alas! we do like cowbirds and cuckoos, which lay their eggs in nests which other birds have built.

Henry David Thoreau, *Walden* 1854

The house-builder at work in cities or anywhere,
The preparatory jointing, squaring, sawing, mortising,
The hoist-up of beams, the push of them in their places, laying them regular,
Setting the studs by their tenons in the mortises, according as they were prepared,
The blows of mallets and hammers, the attitudes of the men, their curv'd limbs,
Bending, standing, astride the beams, driving in pins, holding on by posts and braces,
The hook'd arm over the plate, the other arm wielding the axe,
The floor-men forcing the planks close, to be nail'd,
Their postures bringing their weapons downward on the bearers,
The echoes resounding through the vacant building.

Walt Whitman, *Leaves of Grass* 1855

I count it a duty to make such use of the homely materials at hand, as shall insure durability and comfort, while the simplicity of detail will allow the owner to avail himself of his own labor and ingenuity in the construction. . . .

I may remark here, in way of warning to those who undertake the renovation of slatternly country places with exuberant spirits, that it is a task which often seems easier than it proves.

D. G. Mitchell, *My Farm of Edgewood* 1863

He who digs a well, constructs a stone fountain, plants a grove of trees by the roadside, plants an orchard, builds a durable house, reclaims a swamp, or so much as puts a stone seat by the wayside, makes the land so far lovely and desirable, makes a fortune which he cannot carry away with him, but which is useful to his country long afterwards.

Ralph Waldo Emerson, Farming, in Society and Solitude 1870

It is a great thing to build the house that is to be one's home. There are few pleasures so unalloyed as that of selecting the ground, laying the foundation, and watching day by day the growth of wall and roof that go to form one's secure kingdom through the years to come.

E. H. Leland, Farm Homes 1881

When I set out to look up a place in the country, I was chiefly intent on finding a few acres of good fruitland near a large stone-heap. While I was yet undecided about the land, the discovery of the stone-heap at a convenient distance, vast piles of square blocks of all sizes, wedged off the upright strata by the frost during uncounted ages, and all mottled and colored by the weather, made me hasten to close the bargain. Only a few of the early settlers had availed themselves of this beautiful material that lay in such abundance handy to every man's back door. . . .

It seems to me that I built into my house every one of those superb autumn days which I spent in the woods getting out stone. . . . Every load that was sent home carried my heart and happiness with it. The jewels I had uncovered in the debris, or torn from the ledge in the morning, I saw in the jambs, or mounted high on the corners at night. Every day was filled with great events. The woods held unknown treasures. Those elder giants, frost and rain, had wrought industriously; now we would unearth from the leaf-mould an ugly customer, a stone with a ragged quartz face, or cavernous, and set with rock crystals like great teeth, or else suggesting a battered and worm-eaten skull of some old stone dog. Then we would unexpectedly strike upon several loads of beautiful blocks all in a nest; or we would assault the ledge in a new place with wedge and bar, and rattle down headers and stretchers that surpassed any before.

I had to be constantly on the lookout for corner stone, for mine is a house of seven corners, and on the strength and dignity of the corners the beauty of the wall largely depends. . . . I looked upon the ground with such desire that I saw what was beneath the moss and the leaves. . . . With me it was a passionate pursuit; the enthusiasm of the chase venting itself with the bar and hammer, and the day was too short for me to tire of the sport.

John Burroughs, *Signs and Seasons* 1886

There is nothing obtrusive about old cottages. They do not dominate the landscape, but are content to be part of it, and to pass unnoticed unless one looks specially for their homely beauties. The modern house, on the other hand, makes a bid for your notice. It is built on high ground, commands a wide range of country, and is seen from far and wide. But the old cottage prefers to nestle snugly in shady valleys. The trees grow closely about it in an intimate, familiar way, and at a little distance only the wreath of curling smoke tells of its presence. . . .

In one respect old cottages are like old ballads; we have no idea who their authors were. They belong to the countryside, and seem just to have grown there, tinged and coloured by all the local influences of soil and climate. Their architect was the villager carpenter, for builder and carpenter were the same, when wood was the chief material employed.

Stewart Dick, *The Cottage Homes of England* 1909

The frame house and log house molder and pass away even in the building time, and this makes a proper bond of sympathy and fellowship between the man and his home; but the stone house remains always the same to the person born in it; in his old age it is still as hard, and indifferent, and unaffected by time. . . . The stone house is not of his evanescent race, it has no kinship with him, nor any interest in him.

Mark Twain, *Europe and Elsewhere* 1923

The owner who sends far overland for unusual marbles or granites with which to build his house does not thereby achieve individuality, but the one who, for reasons of economy, digs up the forgotten local stone of the country—he does!

Edwin Bonta, The Small-House Primer 1925

In the home-built house, life goes on enriched by a sense of beauty and an innate dignity that are left over from an older time, when hard work and infinite care, not money, were spent to beautify a house and its furnishings.

K. and D. N. S., Adobe Notes 1930

Nature, to my mind, gave man three materials, to serve him in the course of his life: earth, in which to grow food; wood, from which to fashion furniture; and stone, of which to build his home.

Frazier Peters, Houses of Stone 1933

A culture begins with simple things—with the way the potter moulds the clay on his wheel, the way a weaver threads his yarns, the way the builder builds his house. Greek culture did not begin with the Parthenon: it began with a white-washed hut on a hillside.

Herbert Read, The Politics of the Unpolitical 1943

A man's character emerges in the building and ordering of his house.

Richard Weaver, Ideas Have Consequences 1948

Woodlots and Fire-Making

That fire is best, which is made of drie and sweet wood. For wet and greene wood is discommodious; and so are coales, because they make the head heavie, and dry up naturall moysture.

William Vaughan, *Naturall & Artificial Directions for Health* 1600

Though it bee here somewhat cold in the winter, yet we have plenty of Fire to warm us, and that a great deale cheaper than they sel Billets and Faggots in London; nay, all Europe is not able to afford to make so great Fires as New-England. A poore Servant here that is to possesse but fifty Acres of Land, may afford to give more wood for Timber and Fire, as good as the world yeelds, than many Noblemen in England can afford to do. Here is good living for those that love good Fires.

Francis Higginson, *New-England's Plantation* 1630

A tree: the grandest and most beautiful of all the productions of the earth.

William Gilpin, *Remarks on Forest Scenery* 1791

The duty of a forester consists in preserving order and beauty, furnishing timber or copse, and providing a succession of young trees for falls of timber, additional plantations, other uses, or decay or accident in any part under his charge.

J. C. Loudon, *A Treatise on Forming, Improving & Managing Country Residences* 1806

Let thy fuel be dry, not wet or green: otherwise, you use one fire to dry the wood that is to make another. . . . I have often seen near a quarter of a cord of wood put on the fire to boil a tea-kettle.

Thomas Cooper, *A Treatise of Domestic Medicine* 1824

A cook has many trials of her temper, but none so difficult to bear as the annoyance of a bad fire; for with a bad fire she is never able to cook her dinner well, however much she may fret herself in the endeavour.

Francis Harriet McDougall, *The Housekeeper's Book* 1837

There are few farms in the United States where it is not convenient and profitable to have one or more wood-lots attached. They supply the owner with his fuel, which he can prepare at his leisure; they furnish him with timber for buildings, rails, posts, and for his occasional demands for implements; they require little attention, and if well managed, yield more or less forage for cattle and sheep. The trees should be kept in a vigorous, growing condition, as the profits are as much enhanced from this cause as any of the cultivated crops. . . .

In almost every instance, if the germs of forest vegetation have not been extinguished in the soil, the wood-lot may be safely left to self-propagation, as it will be certain to produce those trees which are best suited to the present state of the soil. . . . In most woodlands nature is left to assert her own unaided preferences, growing what and how she pleases, and it must be confessed she is seldom at variance with the owner's interest. . . .

In cutting over woodlands, it is generally best to remove all the large trees on the premises at the same time. This admits a fresh growth on an equal footing, and allows that variety to get the ascendancy to which the soil is best suited.

R. L. Allen, *The American Farm Book* 1849

The careful manager attends to three things: not to let the fire go so low as to require sticks and bellows to draw it up; always to use the least expensive thing that will burn and answer the purpose required; and always to make a good use of a fire when it is burning.

Esther Copley, *Cottage Cookery* 1850

It is a sad waste to put fuel under a boiling pot. There is a degree of heat in water called the boiling point; and all the coals or wood in the world cannot make water hotter in an open vessel; it can but boil.

Sarah Josepha Hale, *The Ladies' New Book of Cookery* 1852

I found chopping, in the summer months, very laborious. I should have underbrushed my fallow in the fall, before the leaves fell, and chopped the large timber during the winter months, when I should have had the warm weather for logging and burning, which should be completed by the first day of September. So, for want of experience, it was all up-hill work with me.

Samuel Strickland, *Twenty-seven Years in Canada West* 1853

The greatest value is received before the wood is teamed home. . . . It warms us twice, and the first warmth is the most wholesome and memorable, compared with which the other is mere coke. . . . Every man looks at his wood-pile with a kind of affection.

Henry David Thoreau, *Walden* 1854

Lumbermen in their winter camp, day-break in the woods,
Stripes of snow on the limbs of trees, the occasional snapping.
The glad clear sound of one's own voice, the merry song,
The natural life of the woods, the strong day's work,
The blazing fire at night, the sweet taste of supper,
The talk, the bed of hemlock boughs, and the bear-skin. . . .
The log at the wood-pile, the axe supported by it,
The sylvan hut, the vine over the doorway, the space clear'd for a
      garden.

Walt Whitman, *Song of the Broad-Axe* 1856

Have your kindling wood short, and all in a close pile over your crumpled paper. If it is set up like a stack, all the better to ignite.

Solon Robinson, *How to Live* 1860

We piled, with care, our nighly stack
Of wood against the chimney-back,—
The oaken log, green, huge, and thick,
And on its top the stout back-stick;
The knotty forestick laid apart,
And filled between with curious art
The ragged brush; then, hovering near,
We watched the first red blaze appear,

Heard the sharp crackle, caught the gleam
On whitewashed wall and sagging beam,
Until the old-rude-furnished room
Burst, flower-like, into rosy bloom.

Shut in from all the world without
We sat the clean-winged hearth about,
Content to let the north-wind roar
In baffled rage at pane and door,
While the red logs before us beat
The frost-line back with tropic heat;
And ever, when a louder blast
Shook beam and rafter as it passed,
The merrier up its roaring draught
The great throat of the chimney laughed.

John Greenleaf Whittier, Snow Bound 1866

Use green wood for logs, and mix green and dry wood for the fire.
Then the wood-pile will last much longer. . . . Have all your wood
split and piled under cover for winter. Have the green wood logs in
one pile, dry wood in another, oven wood in another, kindlings and
chips in another.

Catherine E. Beecher, The New Housekeeper's Manual 1874

A careful housewife will only use half as much wood or shavings to
start her fire with as a thriftless one, because she will take trouble to
learn that there is a scientific but perfectly simple mode of laying and
lighting a fire.

Lady Barker, First Lessons in the Principles of Cooking 1875

And now you're married, you must be good,
And keep your wife in kindling wood.

Mrs. A. M. Diaz, Hearth and Home 1875

The capacious fire place held an eighth of a cord of wood without
crowding it. In the rear would be placed a large green log, generally of

beech or maple, sometimes two feet in diameter. On top of this a smaller log and a still smaller one above that made the backing. The andirons were then placed in position in front of the back log, the coals raked along in front of it also, and a rousing big forestick laid on the said andirons in front of the fire. Between this and the backing, dry pine and chips would be crammed for kindling, and green wood, if we had no other, which was often the case, piled on top of the whole till a huge pile would be in position.

A good draft would soon set the drier wood burning, the green wood would gradually become roasted dry, and burning slowly, send out a tremendous heat, so that in a half hour you could sit comfortably in the rear of the cabin, and the blazing fire so illuminated the interior that no other light was necessary.

Such fires could only be enjoyed where there was a surplus of forest timber to be destroyed, as was then the case, for it took fifty or more cords a year to feed the kitchen fire alone.

William Reed, *Life on the Border* 1882

I am aware that I shall tell some well known facts, and that many of my readers will say, "Surely, every school girl knows how to make a fire"; yet it is astonishing how many young married women there are, who do not know very simple things. How should they know, so many of them just leave boarding school to pass a few gay months and then marry? I want to leave no margin for what anyone knows or ought to know, and I hope the more experienced will pardon what is to them a thrice told tale.

Catherine Owen, *Progressive Housekeeping* 1889

According to the common estimate of farmers, the woodlot yields its gentle rent of six percent, without any care or thought, when the owner sleeps or travels, and it is subject to no enemy but fire.

Ralph Waldo Emerson, *Country Life* 1893

The agent most essential for any kind of cooking is a fire. The most easily made is one of dry brushwood, but this will only burn for a short time, unless the wood be constantly resupplied. To make such a fire most lasting, it is necessary to feed it with thicker wood, split logs, or faggots. With the aid of such a simple fire on the hearthstones, we can prepare some simple articles of food in a direct manner. We can grill meat before it, by holding it on a stick near the flame or live coal; we can imbed sundry tubers, such as potatoes, fungi such as mushrooms and truffles, or onions, in the ashes, and let them get cooked; or we can heat stones, and, when they are suitably hot, bake upon them a prepared flour-paste, such as that which yields chuppaties. All these elementary modes of cooking should be well studied by travellers, explorers, colonists, soldiers, and sailors.

J. L. W. Thudicum, *The Spirit of Cookery* 1895

The great tree is cut down. It is done, and a change has come over the landscape; the space that for generations has been filled with leafy branches is now white and empty air. I know of no more melancholy sight—indeed, to this day I detest seeing a tree felled; it always reminds me of the sudden and violent death of a man.

H. Rider Haggard, *A Farmer's Year* 1899

No chimpanzee knows how to use fire or to cook a meal. All savages have mastered both arts.

Robert H. Lowie, *Are We Civilized?* 1929

How can I turn from any fire on any man's hearth-stone? I know the wonder and desire that went to build my own.

Rudyard Kipling, *Something of Myself* 1937

There is a good deal of difference between a timber forest and an ideal farm woodlot. The latter must serve a variety of needs. The more different kinds of wood it contains, the better; and there should be trees of all sizes and ages, so that the production of available material for various uses will be steady. Our biggest single need is for firewood. Although we use four fireplaces pretty steadily from early fall into later spring we have seldom had to cut up a whole mature tree for fuel alone: weed trees, fallen trees, and the topwood of trees cut for posts or other purposes supply ninety percent of it.

Henry Tetlow, *We Farm for a Hobby and Make It Pay* 1938

If a man cannot start a cooking fire, he can always locate a Boy Scout to do it for him.

Frank Shay, *The Best Men are Cooks* 1941

"You know, you eat out of that stove and there's a hell of a difference between eatin' out of that stove and eatin' out of an electric or a gas one. It's the smoke in that thing, you know. It flavors the food. Baking beans in that, there's no comparison. Your bread, your biscuits, and everything all taste better on that old stove."

Carol Hill and Bruce Davidson, *Subsistence U.S.A.* 1973

I am the warmth of the hearth on cold winter nights. I am the shade screening you from the summer sun. My fruits and restoring drinks quench your thirst as you journey onward. I am the beam that holds your house; the door of your homestead; the bed on which you lie; and the timber that builds your boat. I am the handle of your hoe, the wood of your cradle, and the shell of your coffin.

Sign on a tree in a public park in Madrid, Spain

Planning and Management

He is wyse, in my conceyte, that wyll have, or he do sette up his howseholde, two or thre yeares rent in his cofer.

Andrewe Boorde, *A Dyetary of Helth* 1542

What husbandlie husbands, except they be fooles,
But handsome have storehouse, for trinkets and tooles:
And all in good order, fast lock'd to ly,
Whatever is needfull, to find by and by.
Things thus set in order, in quiet and rest
Shall further thy harvest and pleasure thee best.

Thomas Tusser, *Five Hundreth Pointes of Good Husbandrie* 1557

Book keeping is certainly very Necessary to all, and without which no person of Bussiness can easily understand the State of his affairs. At all times 'tis Convenient to keep within Bounds, and never let the Disbursements exceed the Profit. Tho his Profits may Ballance his Expence, yet seeing some Extraordinary Accidents may happen, 'tis necessary that his Expence should be some less than his Profits, it being conveniant as the proverb is, that something be keeped for the forefoot. . . . If he find that his Outgivings be greater than what he Receives, he must of Necessity Retrensh his Spending, and proportion it to what he gets in, or otherwise he cannot expect to continue in any Tolerable Condition.

James Donaldson, *The Undoubted Art of Thriving* 1700

As far as you can possibly, pay ready money for everything you buy, and avoid bills. . . . Where you must have bills (as for meat and drink, clothes, etc.), pay them regularly every month, and with your own hand. Never, from a mistaken economy, buy a thing you do not want because it is cheap, or, from a silly pride, because it is dear. Keep an account in a book of all that you receive, and of all that you pay; for no man, who knows what he receives and what he pays, ever runs out.

Earl of Chesterfield, *Letters to His Son* January 10, 1749

Useful Arts are sometimes lost for want of being put into Writing. Tradition is a very slippery Tenure, and a slender Pin to bear any great Weight for a long Time. . . . Whoever has made any observation or Discoveries, altho' it be but a Hint, and looks like a small Matter, yet if pursued and improved, may be of publick Service. . . . I am sure I should have been glad of such an History of Facts (as imperfect as it is). It would have afforded me Light, Courage and Instruction.

Jared Eliot, Essays upon Field-Husbandry in New-England 1760

All gentlemen who make agriculture their business or amusement, should register their trials and either publish them themselves, or communicate them to others who will take that trouble. It is inconceivable how much the world would be benefited by such a conduct; matters relative to rural economics would receive a new face; every day would bring forth some valuable discovery, and every year that passed yield such an increase of knowledge, as to point and smooth the way to discoveries now unthought of. . . . Experiments that are made with spirit and accuracy are of incomparable value in every branch of natural philosophy; those of agriculture, which is the most useful of those branches, must be particularly valuable.

Arthur Young, Rural Economy 1792

There is not a single step in the life of a farmer that does not prove the advantage of his keeping regular accounts; and yet there is not one in a thousand who does it. . . . Every work for the next day is to be arranged, whether for fine or rainy weather, and the farm-books to be made up for the transactions of the past day. Beside these, he should have another book for miscellaneous observations, queries, speculations and calculations, for turning and comparing different ways of effecting the same object. . . . Loose pieces of paper are generally lost after a time, so that when a man wants to turn to them to examine a subject formerly estimated or discussed, he loses more time in searching for a memorandum, than would be sufficient for making half a dozen new ones; but if such matters are entered in a book, he easily finds what he wants, and his knowledge will be in a much clearer progression, by recurring to former ideas and experience.

Arthur Young, The Farmer's Calendar 1805

I have committed follies which I have not forgot. When I went first into the Woods I was as bigoted to the methods I had been used to observe in Pennsylvania, as these Europeans were to theirs. . . . I found fault with their fences. I cavilled at the construction of their waggons, and their geer. I condemned their tools and farming implements. I talked much and to little purpose—they continued their own practices, and I found, after some time, that I had nothing better to do than to conform. . . . What is most in use will be found to be pretty nearly what is best. . . . A wise stranger would be much apter to conform at once to their usages than to begin by teaching them better. . . . I think it safer that the philosopher should learn from the farmer, than the farmer from the philosopher.

William Cooper, *A Guide in the Wilderness* 1810

No man is born in possession of the art of living, any more than of the art of agriculture; the one requires to be studied as well as the other, and a man can no more expect permanent satisfaction from actions performed at random, than he can expect a good crop from seeds sown without due regard to soil and season. . . . Nothing is more conducive to happiness, than fixing on an end to be gained, and then steadily pursuing its attainment. . . .

Whoever intends to embrace farming as a profession, will be less likely to meet with disappointment, if he previously examines a little into his own disposition and talents; and weighs his expectations against ordinary results. Nor is it less essential that he should estimate justly the extent to which his capital may be adequate, and keep regular accounts.

J. C. Loudon, *An Encyclopedia of Agriculture* 1825

For want of records, much useful knowledge is continually lost. Though many individuals have derived advantages to themselves from experiments, but few have recorded them. Even those who make experiments are liable to forget them, so as to give incorrect representations of them when they attempt to relate them.

Leonard E. Lathrop, *The Farmer's Library* 1826

A farmer, by the nature of things, ought to be a man of strict economy. His aim ought to be habitually to prevent waste, in anything, and in all things. After he has paid $70 for his ox wagon, and $45 for the cart, they should not be left exposed to the ardent sun, nor to the rain, but carefully housed under sheds, when not in use. Plough and tools should be secured in the same way.

J. M. Gourgas, in *The New England Farmer* January 25, 1828

I would encourage every family to live within their means. If there be a way—and such a way there certainly is—of living as comfortably and happily, on very small means, as we now do on much larger ones, it is certainly desirable to know it, especially in times like the present. "But suppose the means are very small, what then?" Why, then, live within very small means.

William A. Alcott, *Ways of Living on Small Means* 1837

A limited fortune is no excuse for deficiency in neatness.

Charlotte Gilman, *The Lady's Annual Register* 1838

Were it left to my choice to say which of two things the world should have—the right sort of household management and education, with no school instruction whatever, or the best sort of school education of every grade but without anything done in the household beyond what is now done by 9/10s if not 19/20s of mankind, I should not hesitate a moment to decide on the former. Such is the value I attach to the domestic institution and the family school; and such are my conceptions of the native dignity of house-keeping.

William A. Alcott, *The Young House-Keeper* 1838

Who ever knew a good farmer, of prudent habits, to fail?

John L. Blake, *Farmer's Every Day Book* 1850

That aim in life is highest which requires the highest and finest discipline.

Henry David Thoreau, *Journal* December 28, 1852

If one would live simply and eat only the crop which he raised, and raise no more than he ate, and not exchange it for an insufficient quantity of more luxurious and expensive things, he would need to cultivate only a few rods of ground, and it would be cheaper to spade up that than to use oxen to plough it. He could do all his necessary farm work as it were with his left hand at odd hours in the summer; and would not be tied to an ox, or horse, or cow, or pig, as at present.

Henry David Thoreau, *Walden* 1854

The general management of a garden, whether it includes the pleasure-ground, and all the scenes which come under the gardeners' department in an extensive country residence, or merely a few rods of ground for growing culinary crops and flowers, requires such constant attention throughout the year, that gardeners have wisely invented calendars to remind them of their duty, monthly and even weekly.

J. C. Loudon, *The Horticulturist* 1860

Every farmer should be a merchant as well as farmer; keeping a regular set of books, with plenty of leisure to keep his accounts, make his figures, study the principles of his business, investigate the science of Agriculture for himself, instruct his children, tend to the sale of his goods, which should always be done at home, on his own premises; be his own expert, knowing the cost of everything he produces, that which he consumes as well as what he sells; the whole amount of sales made, the interest on the capital, the taxes, insurance, and the depreciation in value, if any. I know that this will take time, but what of that?

T. J. Pinkham, *Farming As It Is* 1860

There are not a few entertaining people of the cities, who imagine that a farm of one or two hundred acres has a way of managing itself, and that it works out crops and cattle from time to time, very much as small beer works into a foamy ripeness, by a law of its own necessity. I wish with all my heart that it were true; but it is not. For successful farming, there must be a well digested plan of operations, and the faithful execution of that plan.

D. G. Mitchell, *My Farm of Edgewood* 1863

Whatever you do, don't get yourself into a muddle, surrounded by dirty plates, dirty knives, spoons, saucepans and the kitchen table littered all over with bottles, pots, jars, etc. Before commencing to serve dinner, as much as possible, clear up the kitchen.

A. G. Payne, *Choice Dishes at Small Cost* 1882

There are two ways of living: a man may be casual and simply exist, or constructively and deliberately try to do something with his life. The constructive idea implies constructiveness not only about one's own life, but about that of society, and the future possibilities of mankind.

Julian Huxley, *Essays of a Biologist* 1923

Everything depends both on what has been and what is to be. Which suggests the need for a good system of records. Now here I am something of a crank. Many people esteem record-keeping a fifth wheel or fancy flourish on the tail end of any undertaking. Yet I never saw the project, however devised or executed, that would not respond to the treatment that can be prescribed on the evidence of the records. No memory can be trusted, not alone over long periods of time, but from day to day. . . . It is not the fellow weeding the onions in July who is getting the most out of his farm: it is the man who, in January, is planning what kinds and quantities of onions to plant next Spring.

It may be possible to run a farm well without the help of a carefully worked out plan, but if it is, I have never seen it done. . . . The first and most important job in any garden is laying it out on paper, marking in each row the succession of plantings, calculating the amounts of seeds needed, and writing up the seed order. To do this the record of the last year's crops and plantings, as well as the copy of the last seed order, are extremely helpful. The order shows not only the quantity but the variety of each kind of seed bought.

Henry Tetlow, *We Farm for a Hobby and Make It Pay* 1938

I cannot conceive of a good life which isn't, in some sense, a self-disciplined life.

Philip Toynbee, in *The Observer Review* July 18, 1976

Money and True Wealth

There are no riches above a sound body, and no joy above the joy of the heart.

A good wife, and health, are a man's best wealth.

Contentment is the philosopher's stone, which turns all it toucheth into gold; the poor man is rich with it, the rich man poor without it.

Riches consists not in the extent of possessions but in the fewness of wants.

Anonymous, Proverbs for Daily Living undated

It is true that to obtain money by trade is sometimes more profitable, were it not so hazardous; and likewise lending money at interest, if it were an honorable occupation.

Cato the Censor, De Agricultura 160 B.C.

When Cato was asked what was most profitable in the way of property, he replied, "Good pasture." And when the man who asked the question said, "What about lending at interest?" Cato answered, "What about manslaughter?"

Cicero, De Officiis 44 B.C.

Arise, come, hasten, let us abandon the city to merchants, attorneys, brokers, usurers, tax-gatherers, scriveners, doctors, perfumers, butchers, cooks, bakers and tailors, alchemists, painters, mimes, dancers, lute-players, quacks, panderers, thieves, criminals, adulterers, parasites, foreigners, swindlers and jesters, gluttons who with scent alert catch the odor of the market place, for whom that is the only bliss, whose mouths are agape for that alone.

Francesco Petrarch, De Vita Solitaria 1356

We are now come to the last prerogative which in this short discourse we shall reckon for the country-inhabitants, and that is this: they can with lesse charge maintaine their families, and better their estates, than it can be done in cities and courts; for it is well known at what vast and unreasonable expences they live at court, especially in this age, wherein the excessive charge of rich habits and a luxurious diet is grown to such a height, both in courts and cities, that it seems to call for not only the censure of the earthly magistrate, but the divine judgement itself.

Don Antonio de Guevara, *The Praise & Happiness of the Countrie-Life* 1539

Seek not proud riches, but rather such as thou mayest get justly, use soberly, distribute cheerfully, and leave contentedly.

Sir Francis Bacon, *Essay* 1597

There are some People that care for none of these Things, that will enter into no new Scheme, nor take up any other Business than what thay have been enured to, unless you can promise Mountains of Gold.

Jared Eliot, *Essays upon Field-Husbandry in New-England* 1760

These countrymen in general are a very happy people; they enjoy many of the necessities of life upon their own farms, and what they do not so gain, they have from the sale of their surplus products; it is remarkable to see such numbers of these men in a state of great ease and content, possessing all the necessaries of life, but few of the luxuries of it. Their farms yield food—much of cloathing—most of the articles of building—with a surplus sufficient to buy such foreign luxuries as are necessary to make life passably comfortable: there is very little elegance among them—but more of necessaries.

Anonymous, *American Husbandry* 1775

Good people, hark ye: A few rules well observed, will contribute much to your happiness and independence. Never buy what you do not really want. Never purchase on credit what you can possibly do without. Take pride in being able to say, I owe no man.

Poor Robert, *Essays* 1796

In place of the risk and uncertainties of commerce, the country dweller enjoys the less fleeting products of the soil.

> J. C. Loudon, *A Treatise on Forming, Improving & Managing Country Residences* 1806

It is not large funds that are wanted, but a constant supply, like a small stream that never dies. To have a great capital is not so necessary as to know how to manage a small one and never be without a little.

> William Cooper, *Guide in the Wilderness* 1810

The business of the year is done by barter, without the intervention of scarcely a dollar; and thus also we live with a plenty of everything except money.

> Thomas Jefferson, *Letter to Colonel William Duane* March 28, 1811

To provide a good living for himself and family is the very first duty of every man.

> William Cobbett, *Cottage Economy* 1824

The numerous benefits resulting to every family from the productions of a well-cultivated garden are too evident to need any remarks by way of illustration. The health they afford to the family, not only in the luxuries which they furnish for the table; but, in the exercise, amusement and enjoyment they impart in the cultivation, exceed all description. In fact, the fruits and vegetables of a garden are the life of a family, upon every principle of enjoyment and economy; to say nothing of the convenient profit it affords to those who are situated within reach of a market, for any surplus they may have to spare.

> John Randolph, *Randolph's Culinary Gardener* 1826

Gardening is not only an innocent and healthy, but a profitable occupation. It is not alone by the money which is *made*, but also by the money which is *saved*, that the profits of a pursuit should be estimated.

> Thomas G. Fessenden, *The New American Gardener* 1828

No man in this world, however high may be his rank, great his wealth, powerful his genius, or extensive his requirements, can ever attain more than health, enjoyment and respect.

> J. C. Loudon, *The Suburban Gardener* 1838

The rich man is always sold to the institution which makes him (or keeps him) rich. Absolutely speaking, the more money the less virtue; for money comes between a man and his objects. . . . The opportunities of living are diminished in proportion as what are called the "means" are increased. The best thing a man can do for his culture when he is rich is to endeavor to carry out those schemes which he entertained when he was poor.

> Henry David Thoreau, *On the Duty of Civil Disobedience* 1849

For a man to pride himself on this kind of wealth, as if it enriched him, is as ridiculous as if one struggling in the ocean with a bag of gold on his back should gasp out, "I am worth a hundred thousand dollars!" I see his ineffectual struggles just as plainly, and what it is that sinks him.

> Henry David Thoreau, *Journal* November 5, 1857

There are more insane persons than are called so, or are under treatment in hospitals. The crowd in the cities, at the hotels, theatres, card-tables, the speculators who rush for investment, at 10 percent, 20 percent, are all more or less mad.

> Ralph Waldo Emerson, *Country Life* 1858

Wealth begins in a tight roof that keeps the rain and wind out; in a good pump that yields you plenty of sweet water, in dry sticks to burn, in a good double-wick lamp and three meals. . . . Money often costs too much, and power and pleasure are not cheap.

> Ralph Waldo Emerson, *Wealth*, in *The Conduct of Life* 1860

The art of becoming "rich," in the common sense, is not absolutely nor finally the art of accumulating much money for ourselves, but also of contriving that our neighbors shall have less. In accurate terms, it is "the art of establishing the maximum inequality in our own favour." . . .

Perhaps the final outcome and consummation of all wealth is in the producing as many as possible full-breathed, bright-eyed, and happy-hearted human creatures. Our modern wealth, I think, has rather a tendency the other way.

John Ruskin, *Unto This Last* 1862

The innocence of this country life is the next thing for which I commend it. . . . They live by what they can get by industry from the earth; and others, by what they can catch by craft from men. They live upon an estate given them by their mother; and others, upon an estate cheated from their brethren. They live, like sheep and kind, by the allowances of nature; and others, like wolves and foxes, by the acquisition of rapine.

Abraham Cowley, *Essays* 1868

That man is richest whose pleasures are the cheapest.

Henry David Thoreau, *Journal* 1886

For money enters into two different characters into the scheme of life. A certain amount, varying with the number and empire of our desires, is a true necessary to each one of us in the present order of society; but beyond that amount, money is a commodity to be bought or not to be bought, a luxury in which we may either indulge or stint ourselves, like any other. And there are many luxuries that we may legitimately prefer to it, such as a grateful conscience, a country life, or the woman of our inclination.

Robert Louis Stevenson, *Men and Books* 1888

Money is that which passes freely from hand to hand throughout the community, in final discharge of debts and full payment for commodities, being accepted equally without reference to the character or credit of the person who offers it, and without the intention of the person who receives it to consume it, or enjoy it, or apply it to any other use than, in turn, to tender it to others in discharge of debts or payment for commodities. . . . Money is always a medium; an intermediate thing; a means, not an end. Men take it, not for its own sake, but for what it will bring them; they hold it, not to enjoy it, but to be ready for the moment when they shall part with it to obtain that which they will enjoy.

Francis A. Walker, *Money in Its Relation to Trade and Industry* 1889

If there are people at once rich and content, be assured that they are content because they know how to be so, not because they are rich.

Charles Wagner, *The Simple Life* 1901

In Commerce, work is undertaken in order that the product may *sell*, and so yield a profit; that is all. It is of no moment *what* the product is, or whether good or bad, so long as it fulfills this one condition.

Edward Carpenter, *Non-Governmental Society* 1911

The villagers' economy is natural, rather than monetary; their commerce and finances are incidental rather than dominant powers driving the whole. . . . Though their world has not the power and stimulation that modern times have . . . it has built a value and a deep security of its own.

Baker Brownell, *Earth is Enough* 1933

Whereas it matters little on Medlock Farm whether the cost of living goes up or down—it is not so much the market price of a dozen ears of corn that concerns us as that we have our own corn on the cob. No matter how low it goes it will still be cheaper to grow it than to buy it.

Henry Tetlow, *We Farm for a Hobby and Make It Pay* 1938

Many wealthy people are little more than the janitors of their possessions.

Frank Lloyd Wright, *On Architecture* 1941

All that is really useful to us can be bought for little money; it is only the superfluous that is put up for sale at a high price. All that is really beautiful is not put up for sale at all but is offered us as a gift by the immortal gods. We are allowed to watch the sun rise and set, the clouds sailing along in the sky, the forests and the fields, the glorious sea, all without spending a penny. The birds sing to us for nothing, the wild flowers we may pick as we are walking along by the roadside. There is no entrance fee to the starlit hall of the Night. The poor man sleeps better than the rich. Simple food tastes in the long run better than food from the Ritz. Contentment and peace of mind thrive better in a small country cottage than in the stately palace in a town. A few friends, a few books, indeed a very few, and a dog, is all you need to have about you as long as you have yourself. But you should live in the country. The first town was planned by the Devil.

Axel Munthe, *The Story of San Michele* 1948

The Simple Life
Need Not Be Poverty

How happy is he that owes nothing but to himself, and only that which he can easily refuse or easily pay. I do not reckon him poor that has but a little. . . . . All I desire is that my poverty may not be a burden to myself, or make me so to others; and that is the best state of fortune, that is neither necessitous, nor far from it.

With parsimony, a little is sufficient, and without it, nothing; whereas frugality makes a poor man rich. If we lose an estate, we had better never have had it. He that has least to lose has least to fear; and those are better satisfied whom fortune never favored, than those whom she has forsaken.

He that is not content in poverty would not be so neither in plenty; for the fault is not in the thing, but in the mind. If he be sickly, remove him from a cottage to a palace, he is at the same pass; for he carries his disease along with him. What can be happier than that condition both of mind and of fortune from which we cannot fall? A man may lie as warm and as dry under a thatched as under a gilded roof.

Seneca, Of a Happy Life A.D. 45

O God! methinks it were a happy life
To be no better than a homely swain,
To set upon a hill, as I do now. . . .
So many hours must I tend my flock;
So many hours must I take my rest;
So many hours must I contemplate;
So many hours must I sport myself;
Ah, what a life were this, how sweet! how lovely!

William Shakespeare, Henry the Sixth 1623

I hear the whistling ploughman all day long,
Sweet'ning his labour with a cheerful song;
His bed's a pad of straw, his diet, coarse;
In both, he fares not better than his horse;
He seldom slakes his thirst, but from the pump;

And yet his heart is blithe, his visage plump;
His thoughts are ne'er acquainted with such things
As griefs or fears; he only sweats and sings.

> Francis Quarles, *The Ploughman* 1640

Let not ambition mock their useful toil;
their homely joys, and destiny obscure;
Nor grandeur hear with a disdainful smile
the short and simple annals of the poor.

> Thomas Gray, *Elegy Written in a Country Churchyard* 1751

Homeward he hies, enjoys that clean coarse food
Which, season'd with good humour, his fond bride
'Gainst his return is happy to provide.
Short are his meals, and homely is his fare;
His thirst he slakes at some pure neighborhood brook,
Nor asks for sauce where appetite stands cook.

> Charles Churchill, *The Villager* 1760

What though on hamely fare we dine,
Wear hodden grey, an' a' that?
Gie fools their silks, an' knaves their wine,
A man's a man for a' that!

> Robert Burns, *For A' That An' A' That* 1790

The Americans are not accustomed to what we call grand feasts; they treat strangers as they treat themselves every day, and they live well. They say they are not anxious to starve themselves the week, in order to gormandize on Sunday. This trait will paint to you a people at their ease, who wish not to torment themselves for show.

> J. P. Brissot de Warville, *Nouveau Voyage dans les Etats Unis* 1791

Those are happy who have been brought up in the habit of being content with humble fare, whose health is so firm that it needs no artificial adjustment; who, with the appetite of a cormorant, have the digestion of an ostrich and eagerly devour whatever is set before them without asking any questions about what it is or how it has been prepared.

Dr. William Kitchiner, *The Cook's Oracle* 1817

If a Canadian can keep up his supply of pork and pumpkin-pie, of molasses and sourcrout, of tea and Johnny cake,—which he seldom fails to accomplish,—he feels perfectly indifferent regarding those household conveniences which are not so eminently useful.

E. A. Talbot, *Five Years' Residence in the Canadas* 1824

Let it be understood that by poverty I mean real want, a real insufficiency of the food and raiment and lodging necessary to health and decency, and not that imaginary poverty of which some persons complain. The man who, by his own and his family's labour can provide a sufficiency of food and raiment and a comfortable dwelling place, is not a poor man.

William Cobbett, *Cottage Economy* 1824

For all things produced in a garden, whether of salads or fruits, a poor man will eat better that has one of his own, than a rich man that has none.

J. C. Loudon, *An Encyclopedia of Gardening* 1826

His breakfast, water-porridge, humble food:
A barley crust he in his wallet flings;
On this he toils and labours in the wood,
And chops his faggot, twists his band, and sings
As happily as princes and as kings,
With all their luxury: blest is he.

John Clare, *The Woodsman* 1830

With respect to luxuries and comforts, the wisest have ever lived a more simple and meagre life than the poor. The ancient philosophers, Chinese, Hindoo, Persian, and Greek, were a class than which none has been poorer in outward riches, none so rich in inward. . . . Simplify, simplify. Instead of three meals a day, if it be necessary, eat but one; instead of a hundred dishes, five; and reduce other things in proportion.

Henry David Thoreau, *Walden* 1854

By poverty, i.e. simplicity of life and fewness of incidents, I am solidified and crystallized, as a vapor or liquid by cold. It is a singular concentration of strength and energy and flavor. . . . By simplicity, commonly called poverty, my life is concentrated and so becomes organized.

Henry David Thoreau, *Journal* February 8, 1857

In almost every case where a young man has bought a farm, and has been temperate and industrious and had tolerable health, he has made money. They have most of them good, comfortable dwellings, well-painted inside and out, for their families, good barns for their stock, and sheds for wood, carriages, grain, etc., most of which they have either built or repaired since they came into their possession. They educate their children, and spend money for proper purposes as freely as any other class of citizens.

T. J. Pinkham, *Farming As It Is* 1860

[Thoreau] had no talent for wealth, and knew how to be poor without the least hint of squalor or inelegance. . . . He chose to be rich by making his wants few, and supplying them himself.

Ralph Waldo Emerson, *Thoreau* 1862

"No man is rich," says Judge Haliberton, "whose expenditure exceeds his income, and no one is poor whose income exceeds his outgoings."

R. K. Philp, *The Domestic World* 1878

Life to millions is a hardship from labor and poverty; to others a curse through vices and the depravities of wealth; to a few a blessing through good health, good nature and facile contentment, and in this class your humble servant belongs. Always ready to work; never chained, Ixion-like, to the wheel of traffic; comfortable with small earnings, the result of early drill and self-denial made easy from habit, he has plodded along, quite unambitious for wealth; regardless of fame; earnest in acquisition of knowledge on a small scale; rather careful not to know too much; quite sceptical as to believing fashionable lies, and always punctual in paying debts.

William Reed, *Life on the Border* 1882

To be poor may be a misfortune, but it is not a fault. What does it matter if some may sneer at your thread-bare carpets and frugal fare? The discipline of poverty and the self-denial it involves will often strengthen a character which the luxury of riches would enervate.

Mary Harrison, *The Skilful Cook* 1884

If greater peace and better temper are found in cabins than in palaces, it is because comfort is more uncommon in the palace than it is in the cabin. Amidst all their wealth the unfortunates do not know how to live!

E. P. de Senancour, *Obermann* 1903

To possess one small fragment of the world's surface; to have a hut, a cabin or a cottage that was verily my own, to eat the fruits of my own labour on the soil—this seemed to me the crown and goal of all human felicity.

W. J. Dawson, *The Quest of the Simple Life* 1907

The chief necessity of the pioneers was a shelter for their families. The rudest of log cabins were the first abodes, and these were built by the joint labour of the settlers. Sometimes the cabin would be built around a stump, which could be used as a hand-mill or, by placing some basswood slabs on top, would serve as a table. For these homes, glass was not always obtainable and in many cases light was admitted through oiled paper stretched over holds in the walls. The household utensils were of wood—wooden plates, wooden platters, wooden forks, and wooden spoons. In some households forks and knives were unknown and home-made spoons were used instead.

Wild fruit abounded, and this was gathered and either preserved by using maple sugar, or dried for future use. Walnuts, hickory-nuts, butter-nuts, chest-nuts, and beech-nuts were stored up for winter. Honey was obtained from wild bees and maple sugar was made in large quantities every spring. Game was plentiful and each settler had a store of venison and squirrel salted down in barrels made of the hollow trunks of trees. Tea was scarce, a luxury to be used only on state occasions. These first settlers used, as substitutes, sage, sassafras, thyme, spicewood, hemlock, and a wild herb called the tea-plant. "Coffee" was made from peas, barley, acorns, and roots of the dandelion. Physicians were almost unknown, and these pioneers collected and dried medicinal herbs and stored them ahead for time of need.

W. L. Smith, *Pioneers of Ontario* 1923

I do not think that any civilization can be called complete until it has progressed from sophistication to unsophistication, and made a conscious return to simplicity of thinking and living.

Lin Yutang, *The Importance of Living* 1938

The inhabitants of these villages [in Ladak, Tibet] must surely be some of the happiest on the face of the earth. One can only pray that no zealous enthusiast will feel impelled to "raise their standard of living," acting on some sociological theory worked out under totally dissimilar circumstances. Certain writers have alluded to the poverty of the people, doubtless referring to their lack of ready money and their rather Spartan simplicity of life. There is no luxury, nor a big margin of surplus food, but if the enjoyment of a sufficient, if rather unvaried, diet—composed of tasty, unadulterated materials—and the leading of a healthy, outdoor life in majestic surroundings, with work which has its leisured as well as strenuous phases, the wearing of durable and comely homespun clothing, the dwelling in spacious, well-built homes, and the possession of a restricted number of objects pleasing to the eye—if all this be poverty, then let us deplore our wealth!

Marco Pallis, *Peaks and Lamas* 1939

I am against the concept of raising the standard of living endlessly. There will never be a possibility of contentment. Life is larger than bathtubs, radios and refrigerators. These comforts are beneath contempt. I am afraid that the higher the standard of living, the lower the culture.

Ananda K. Coomaraswamy, in *The Aryan Path* August 1947

The lesson which Henry David Thoreau had taught himself and which he hoped he might teach to others was summed up in the one word: "Simplify!" . . . But hearers are not always heeders and very few of Thoreau's professing admirers are willing to accept in its full rigor his central doctrine.

Joseph Wood Krutch, *H. D. Thoreau* 1948

As we live and as we are, Simplicity—with a capital "S"—is difficult to comprehend nowadays. We are no longer truly simple. We no longer live in simple terms or places. Life is a more complex struggle now. It is now valiant to be simple: a courageous thing to even want to be simple. It is a spiritual thing to comprehend what simplicity means.

Frank Lloyd Wright, *The Natural House* 1954

Woman's Place in the Home

I wyll teche a Lesson for the Wyfe: that is, that she shulde not by ydle
at noo tyme: for as in standynge water are engendred wormes, ryghte
soo in an ydle body are engendered ydle thoughtes.

Anonymous, *The Boke of Husbandry* undated

Though husbandrie seemeth to bring in the gaines,
Yet huswiferie labours seeme equal in paines.
Some respite to husbands the weather may send,
But huswives' affairs have never an end.
Wash dishes, lay leavens, save fires and away,
Lock doors and to bed, a good huswife will say.

I serve for a day, for a week, for a year,
For lifetime, forever, while man dwelleth here.
For richer, for poorer, from north to the south,
For honest, for hard head, for dainty of mouth,
For wed and unwed, in sickness and health,
For all that well liveth in good common wealth,
For city, for country, for court, and for cart,
To quiet the head, and comfort the heart.

Thomas Tusser, *Five Hundreth Pointes of Good Husbandry* 1557

The yoongest ladies of the court, when they be at home, can helpe to
supplie the ordinarie want of the kitchen with a number of delicat
dishes of their own devising.

Raphael Holinshed, *The Chronicles of England, Scotlande and Irelande* 1577

To speake then of the outward and active knowledges which belong to
our English Housewife, I hold the first and most principall to be a
perfect skill and knowledge in Cookery, together with all the secrets
belonging to the same, because it is a dutie rarely belonging to the
woman, and she that is utterly ignorant therein may not by the lawes
of strict justice challenge the freedome of Marriage, because indeed
she can then but performe halfe her vow; for she may love and obey,

but shee cannot serve and keepe him without that true dutie which is ever expected.

Gervase Markham, Country Contentments 1615

A good wife is a world of wealth, where just cause of content makes a kingdom in conceit: she is the eye of wariness, the tongue of silence, the hand of labour, and the heart of love: a companion of kindness, a mistress of passion, an exercise of patience, and an example of experience: she is the kitchen physician, the chamber comfort, the hall's care, and the parlour's grace; she is the dairy's neatness, the brewhouse's wholesomeness, the garner's provision, and the garden's plantation: her voice is music, her countenance meekness, her mind virtuous, and her soul gracious: she is her husband's jewel, her children's joy, her neighbor's love, and her servant's honour: she is poverty's prayer, and charity's praise, religion's love, and devotion's zeal: she is a care of necessity, and a course of thrift, a book of housewifery, and a mirror of modesty. In sum, she is God's blessing, and man's happiness, earth's honour and Heaven's creature.

Nicholas Breton, The Good and the Bad 1616

The right Education of the Female Sex, as it is in a manner every where neglected, so it ought to be generally lamented. Most in this depraved later Age think a Woman learned and wise enough if she can distinguish her Husband's Bed from anothers. Vain man is apt to think we were merely intended for the World's propagation, and to keep its humane inhabitants sweet and clean; but by their leaves, had we the same Literature, he would find our brains as fruitful as our bodies.

Hannah Wooley, The Gentlewoman's Companion 1673

The Art of Household Oeconomy is divided, as Xenophon tells us, between the Men and the Women; the Men have the most dangerous and laborious Share of it in the Fields and without Doors, and the Women have the Care and Management of every Business within Doors, and to see to the good ordering of whatever is belonging to the

House. And this, I conceive, is no less the Practice of these Days, than it was in the time of that great Philosopher.

R. Bradley, *The Country Housewife* 1732

If a lady has never been accustomed, while single, to think of family management, let her not upon that account fear that she cannot attain it; she may consult others who are more experienced, and acquaint herself with the necessary quantities of the several articles of family expenditure in proportion to the number it consists of.

Mary Eliza Rundell, *A New System of Domestic Cookery* 1808

The cultivation of talents and habits of economy and usefulness, particularly domestic habits in the female character, are essential to females. The woman who possesses not these qualifications, whatever else she may possess, will never fulfil either with credit to herself, or with satisfaction to others, the important duties of her sex—of a daughter, a wife, a mother or a mistress of a family.

Anonymous, *The Female Instructor, or Young Woman's Companion* 1811

A young lady may learn the delectable Arcana of Domestic Affairs in as little time as is usually devoted to directing the position of her hands on a pianoforte or of her feet in a Quadrille. This will enable her to make the Cage of Matrimony as comfortable as the Net of Courtship was charming.

Dr. William Kitchiner, *The Cook's Oracle* 1817

To understand the Economy of Household Affairs is not only essential to a Woman's proper and pleasant performance of the duties of a Wife and a Mother, but is indispensable to the Comfort, Respectability, and general Welfare of all Families—whatever be their Circumstances.

Dr. William Kitchiner, *The Housekeeper's Ledger* 1825

The resources of her husband may demand from her a rigid adherence to economy, neither easy nor pleasant, when contrary habits and

tastes have, under more liberal circumstances, been fixed and cultivated. Such alterations in habit may at first be regarded as sacrifices,
but in the end they will meet their compensation in the satisfaction
which always results from the consciousness of acting with propriety
and consistency.

Mrs. William Parker, *Domestic Duties* 1828

There was a time when ladies knew nothing *beyond* their own family
concerns; but in the present day there are many who know nothing
about them. Each of these extremes should be avoided.

H. L. Barnum, *Family Receipts* 1831

From my greenest youth, when I used to play about and make
dirt-pies with my brothers and sisters, I had a stirring ambition to be
useful in my generation; and it was ever my opinion as long ago as I
can remember, that nothing in the whole circle of female duties was so
useful and becoming to a modest and virtuous woman as a practical
knowledge of the mysteries of cookery. . . .

Though arrived at the age of discretion, which, in my opinion, no
woman attains under fifty, I have never been married. I spoiled my
complexion by poring over the fire, studying the practical part of the
sublime science, and, like all great cooks that I have ever heard of,
grew fat, as it were, by broiling over the coals. Hence, the idle young
fellows of my acquaintance paid me little attention, and I have been
for many years past left to the unmolested enjoyment of my favorite
pursuit, without any other solace than the proud consciousness that I
was preparing myself to be useful to the great mass of mankind
instead of being subject to the caprices of one alone.

Prudence Smith, *Modern American Cookery* 1831

It is not beneath the solicitude of a good wife, who would not suffer
any abatement in the affection of which she is the object, constantly to
provide a neat and well-dressed repast.

Mrs. N. K. M. Lee, *The Cook's Own Book* 1832

Look you, I keep his house, and I wash, wring, brew, bake, scour, dress meat and drink, make the beds, and do all myself. 'Tis a great charge to come under one body's hand.

Clarissa Packard, *Recollections of a Housekeeper* 1834

The sexes are manifestly intended for different spheres, and constructed in conformity to their respective destinations. But disparity need not imply inferiority.

A knowledge of domestic duties is beyond all price to a woman. Every one of our sex ought to know how to sew, and knit, and mend, and cook, and superintend a household. In every situation of life, high or low, this sort of knowledge is of great advantage.

Useful occupations ought not to be discouraged by the contempt of those who are not obliged to pursue them for a livelihood. It has been held derogatory to the dignity of those who are in the possession of wealth to understand the more humble departments of domestic industry. Hence, their exceeding helplessness, their miserable imbecility, in times of trial, when by fluctuations of fortune or the common accidents of life, they are thrown upon their own resources.

Mrs. L. H. Sigourney, *Letters to Young Ladies* 1835

The young mistress trembles, lest by her inexperience, she should render her husband's table uncomfortable, or extravagantly exceed his resources and plunge him into difficulties.

Esther Copley, *The Housekeeper's Guide* 1838

To see a patient and laborous female spending nearly her whole time in ministering to the mere physical wants of man, in the various stages of his existence—infancy, childhood, youth, manhood and age—and doing all this with the utmost cheerfulness, and without appearing to realize that God has given her a higher and nobler office, is indeed most lamentable. . . . Would that our young females had but an imperfect conception of the power they possess to labor in the cause of human improvement. Would they had but an imperfect idea of female responsibility!

William A. Alcott, The Young Woman's Guide to Excellence 1852

The treadmill routine of the week is: washing, baking, ironing, fixing dried fruit, airing clothes, sewing, cleaning, baking and cleaning again. So it goes week after week. Eating and drinking, cooking and cleaning, scrubbing and scouring we go through life; and only lay down our implements at the verge of the grave! . . . You bake, and boil, and fry, and stew; worry and toil, just as if people's principal business in this world was to learn how much they could eat—and eat it.

Girls, do not scrub and cook and scour until you have no time left to plant a tree, or vine, or flower.

Jane G. Swissholm, Letters to Country Girls 1853

A better time is coming. Women, capable of using their faculties for the improvement of society, will not much longer remain in the castle of indolence. Would that those of my sex who are urging onward, into the industrial pursuits, and other professions appropriate to men, might turn their attention to improvements in domestic economy. Here is an open field, where their heads and hearts as well as hands may find ample scope and noble objects.

Sara Josepha Hale, The New Household Receipt-Book 1853

It will never mar your happiness, affect your dignity, nor deteriorate from your health to digress from your present occupation or accomplishments and acquaint yourselves with domestic economy.

Mrs. M. L. Scott, The Practical Housekeeper & Young Woman's Friend 1855

Here lies a poor woman who always was tired,
For she lived in a place where help wasn't hired.
Her last words on earth were, Dear Friends, I am going
Where washing ain't done, nor sweeping, nor sewing,

And everything there is exact to my wishes,
For there they don't eat; there's no washing of dishes.
Don't mourn for me now, don't mourn for me never,
For I'm going to do nothing forever and ever.

Epitaph on a gravestone in Bushey churchyard 1860

If a young wife be handy with her needles, and has had experience
under her parents' roof, she will find $1000 per annum a sum all-
sufficient to steer her matrimonial craft safely over the shoals and
breakers, provided always that love sits at the helm.

Eliza Warren, *How I Managed My House on $1000 a Year* 1866

God made the woman to do the work of the family. Choose wisely,
then, O youthful mother and housekeeper! Train yourself to wholesome labor and intelligent direction, and be prepared to educate a
cheerful and healthful flock of your own children.

Catherine E. Beecher, *The New Housekeeper's Manual* 1874

Every mother and every wife may regard herself as a vestal priestess
in the temple of existence, and charged with the sacred duty of
keeping the flame ever bright upon the altar of life.

J. B. and L. E. Lyman, *How to Live* 1882

Every woman should face the fact—and consider it intelligently—
that she chose her mission in accepting the hand of a man who, she
knew, could afford to keep neither cook nor chamber maid. And—
having selected it of her own free will—she is bound by honor and
conscience to make the best of it and herself.

Marion Harland, *The Cottage Kitchen* 1883

Too many girls are, unfortunately, imbued with the vulgar notion
that work is not genteel. It would effect a moral revolution if woman
would only look at matters in the true light. Let us hope that the
refinement, falsely so called, which is only another word for vanity,

laziness and selfishness, may soon give way to the true refinement of heart and mind which considers nothing too menial which will benefit others; nothing too common that will add to the happiness of our fellow creatures.

Mary Harrison, The Skilful Cook 1884

Accomplishments, all very good in their way, must, to the true housewife, be secondary to all that concerns the health, the feeding, the clothing, the housing of those under her care. And what a range of knowledge this implies—from sanitary engineering to patching a garment, from bandaging a wound to keeping the frost out of water pipes. It may safely be said that the mistress of a family is called upon to exercise an amount of skill and learning in her daily routine such as is demanded of few men, and this too without the benefit of any special education or preparation.

Spon's Household Manual 1887

The most conventional customs cling to the table. Farmers who wouldn't drive a horse too hard expect pie three times a day.

Ella H. Richards, The Healthful Farmhouse 1906

Nobody pretends that dish-washing is attractive, and nothing but Christian grace makes us endure the pots and pans, but cookery is high art; let us think of it as such, and we shall be properly proud of such triumphs as we achieve. Who would not rather make a delicate strawberry short-cake than play The Maiden's Prayer on the piano? Where is the painted table-scarf that can compare with an honest loaf of milk-white bread?

Kate Douglas Wiggin, A Book of Dorcas Dishes & Family Recipes 1911

The theory that the man who raises corn does a more important piece of work than the woman who makes it into bread is absurd. The inference is that the men alone render useful service. But neither man nor woman eats these things until the woman has prepared it.

Ida M. Tarbell, The Business of Being a Woman 1912

How to Cook a Husband: A good many husbands are entirely spoiled by mismanagement in cooking, and so are not tender and good. Some women keep them too constantly in hot water; others freeze them; others put them in a stew; others keep them constantly in a pickle. It cannot be supposed that any husband will be good and tender if managed in this way. But they are truly delicious if properly treated, agreeing nicely with you, and he will keep as long as you want to have him.

Anonymous, in Bermuda Royal Gazette December 1916

Whoever can toss up, day in and day out, as many meals as may be required, make them edible and varied and as effortless as possible, is a good cook, plenty good enough for you and me. And unsung females are doing just this all the time.

Alexander Wright, How to Live without a Woman 1937

Every day, before breakfast, my mother did the house-work. Her life, like the life of other farmers' wives, was a continual battle against dirt: dirt brought in on the men's feet, red marks where their arms rested on tablecloths, and earth-stains on shirts and overalls and towels and the sheets which, in spite of Father's noisy ablutions, by the end of the week were faintly red. During wet weather, implements carried mud into the yard, already muddy, and the stuff came in on our feet; in dry weather it drifted in as dust. It was all swept away, and on Mondays the washing was well on the way to being hung out, before we sat down to our porridge and cream and piled plates of bacon and eggs and fried potatoes.

Elizabeth Clarke, The Darkening Green 1964

Many women are poor cooks only because their native greatness has been beaten down by ingratitude.

Robert Farrar Capon, The Supper of the Lamb 1969

'Twas the Night before Christmas, or so sayeth the book.
Not a creature was stirring, excepting the Cook.

Anonymous and undated

The Male Point of View

Who can find a virtuous woman?
For her price is far above rubies. . . .
She looketh well to the ways of her household,
And eateth not the bread of idleness.

Proverbs 31:10–27

Wo was his cook, if his sauce were not poynaunt and sharp.

Geoffrey Chaucer, *Canterbury Tales* 1387 ff.

Provide for thy husband, to make him good cheere,
Make merrie together while time ye be heere.
At bed and at boord, howsoever befall,
What ever God sendeth, be merrie withall.

Take weapon away, of what force is a man?
Take huswife from husband, and what is he then?
As lovers desireth together to dwell,
So husbandrie loveth good huswiferie well.

Wife, sometime this week, if the weather hold clear,
An end of wheat sowing we make for this year:
Remember thou therefore, tho I do it not,
The seed cake, the pasties, and furmenty pot.

Good Cooke to dresse dinner to bake and to brewe,
Deserves a reward, being honest and trewe.

Thomas Tusser, *Five Hundreth Pointes of Good Husbandrie* 1557

It was an odde saying of a mad Fellow, who having well dined, clapt
his hand upon the board, and protested, that this eating and drinking
was a very pretty invention, who ever first found it out.

Sir Thomas Mayerne, *Excellent & Approved Experiments in Cookery* 1658

Nothing lovelier can be found in woman, than to study household
goods.

John Milton, *Paradise Lost* 1667

Happy art thou, whom God does bless
With the full choice of thine own happiness;
And happier yet, because thou'rt blest
With prudence, how to choose the best.
In books and gardens thou hast plac'd aright
(Things which thou well dost understand;
And both dost make with thy laborious hand)
Thy noble, innocent delight:
And in thy virtuous wife, where thou again dost meet
Both pleasures more refin'd and sweet:
The fairest garden in her looks,
And in her mind the wisest books.
Oh, who would change these soft, yet solid joys,
For empty shows and senseless noise,
And all which rank ambition breeds,
Which seem such beauteous flowers, and are such poisonous weeds?

Abraham Cowley, *Essays in Verse & Prose* 1668

What a relief to the labouring husband to have a warm comfortable meal!

Maria Eliza Rundell, *A New System of Domestic Cookery* 1807

The influence of cookery on domestic happiness must be evident to all those who have had experience of the toils and troubles of a married life.

Prudence Smith, *Modern American Cookery* 1831

It is cold comfort for a hungry man to tell him how delightfully his wife plays and sings. Lovers may live on very aerial diet, but husbands stand in need of something more solid; and young women may take my word for it that a constantly clean board, well-cooked victuals, a house in order, and a cheerful fire, will do more towards preserving a husband's heart, than all the accomplishments taught in all the establishments in the world.

I do not know, nor can I form an idea of a more unfortunate being than a girl with a mere boarding-school education. Of what use are her accomplishments? Of what use her music, her drawings, and her romantic epistles? If a young man do marry such a girl, let him bear the consequences with good temper. Let him be just, be patient with her, reflect that he has taken her, being apprised of her inability; bear in mind that he was, or seemed to be, pleased with her showy and useless acquirements; and that when the gratification of his passion has been accomplished, he is unjust and cruel and unmanly if he turn round upon her, and accuse her of a want of that knowledge which he well knew that she did not possess.

We discover, when it is too late, that we have not got a help-mate, but a burden; and, the fire of love being damped, the unfortunately educated creature (whose parents are more to blame than she is), unless she revolve to learn her duty is doomed to lead a life very nearly approaching to that of misery; for, however considerate the husband, he never can esteem her as he would have done, had she been skilled and able in domestic affairs.

William A. Alcott, *The Young Man's Guide* 1834

In heaven I hope to bake my own bread and clean my own linen.

Henry David Thoreau, *Journal* March 3, 1841

A kitchen without a female cook is like a flowerless garden, a waveless sea, a sailless ship.

Alexis Soyer, *The Gastronomic Regenerator* 1846

You can hardly call that house a home to which a man dares not carry a friend without previous notice to his wife or daughter, for fear of finding an ill-dressed, ill-served dinner, together with looks of dismay at the intrusion.

A Lady of Charleston, *The Carolina Housewife* 1847

Often has the affectionate wife caused her husband a sleepless night and severe distress because she has prepared for him food which did not agree with his constitution or habits.

Sarah Josepha Hale, *The Ladies' New Book of Cookery* 1852

Around the social board every member of the family is collected thrice at least in 24 hours. Thither the head of the family returns from the labors or cares of his business to recruit his strength and to relax his mind. If he return to a table constantly and invariably ill spread, to a dinner to which he could invite no friend, and in which he can have no enjoyment, a cloud will gather on the calmest brow, and a feeling of dissatisfaction may be extended to other things. It is not beneath the solicitude of a good wife, who would not suffer any abatement in the affection of which she is the object, constantly to provide a neat and well-dressed repast.

A Boston Housekeeper, *The Cook's Own Book* 1854

If there is any class of men that requires regularly good living—victuals palatable, nourishing and well-cooked, it is farmers. They need it, and they deserve it: and, if the woman to whom the responsibility of this preparation belongs, for any trivial cause is negligent, she does not deserve the station she holds.

Rev. John L. Blake, *The Farmer's Every-Day Book* 1854

To your casseroles, then, women of Britain! Turn your thoughts to that art which, coming into action every day in the year, during the longest life, includes within its circles the whole philosophy of economy and order, the presence of good health and of the tone of good society—all within your province.

Charles Pierce, *The Household Manager* 1857

Lord Dudley was so fond of apple pie that he could not dine comfortably without it. On one occasion at a grand dinner he missed his favorite dish and could not resist saying audibly, "God bless my soul! No apple pie!"

Julia C. Andrews, *Breakfast, Dinner & Tea* 1860

If he be by nature indolent, and in temper desponding, easily daunted by difficulties and of a weak frame of body, such a pioneer life would not suit him. If his wife be a weakly woman, destitute of mental energy, unable to bear up under the trials of life, she is not fit for a life of hardship—it will be useless cruelty to expose her to it.

C. P. Traill, *The Canadian Settler's Guide* 1860

I have always thought that there is no more fruitful source of family discontent than a housewife's badly cooked dinner and untidy ways. Men are now so well-served at their clubs, well-ordered taverns, and dining houses, that in order to compete with the attractions of these places, a mistress must be thoroughly acquainted with the theory and practice of cookery, as well as be perfectly conversant with all the other arts of making and keeping a comfortable home.

Isabella Beeton, *The Book of Household Management* 1861

Let her not listen to that mental *ignus fatuus* (foolish fire) "women's rights," but keep her head and heart clear from all that may cause her to lose sight of her true destiny. . . . It is by attention to the domestic duties that this is to be accomplished.

Mrs. Goodfellow's Cookery As It Should Be 1865

Young housekeepers, who, marrying before their domestic education has received sufficient attention, daily find many stumbling blocks in their way, which haply a word fitly spoken might remove. If no part of their child-life was devoted to those lessons, what is the result? The home which the lover dreamed of proves dark and comfortless, and the bride is too often transformed into the heartless devotee of fashion, instead of the companion and helpmeet God designed a wife to be.

Young ladies would soon discover the richer life there is in one's own home if they were early initiated into an intimate knowledge of the whole routine of home duties and household mysteries, so that when they shall be exalted to the dignity of the mistress of a house, they can with good judgment and intelligence direct their servants, or independently perform the labor of a family, easily and methodically, with their own hands. With such knowledge, and the ability to execute, they can greatly augment domestic happiness and add new lustre to their charms as companion and friend.

Catherine E. Beecher, *Motherly Talks with Young Housekeepers* 1873

The idea occurred to me that woman might *not* have been created mainly for the purpose of getting three meals a day.

> A. M. Diaz, *Papers Found in the Schoolmaster's Trunk* 1875

Man wants good dinners. It is woman's province to provide them.

> M. E. W. Sherwood, *The Art of Entertainment* 1892

A tasty, wholesome, nutritious dietary, from day to day, will do much to make a home happy, and whilst it ministers to the pleasures of the moment, its consequences are far-reaching—more so than most people imagine. It will enable the bread-winner to earn his wage with a light heart and with a less exhausted frame, and it will add to the wealth of the family, and thus to the wealth of the States, by the rearing of healthy offspring.

> Martha H. Gordon, *Cookery for Working-Men's Wives* 1898

As most men work all their days from the time they are boys till they are old men, and seldom get any more out of it than a carthorse does—merely harness, food and a bed at night, they have a right to expect that their stable should be comfortable, their bran-mash fit to eat, and their rest undisturbed. All that we ask are comfort and clothes and food. . . .

I do not know any detail of domestic life that I, or any man of my acquaintance, could not manage better than women do, but I am open to conviction of the contrary, if any woman is brave enough to come forward and refute me with proof.

Any man who could give his time to the subject would manage a house, a few servants, and a few children to much greater advantage than any woman.

> A Mere Man, *The Domestic Blunders of Women* 1900

When a well bred girl expects to wed, 'tis well to remember that men like bread.

> Gold Medal Flour advertisement, in *Ladies' Home Journal* April 1903

If satirists and grumbling wives are to be believed, a husband can hardly do a more imprudent thing than to bring home an unexpected guest to dinner, luncheon or supper. But if malcontent Mary but knew it, he pays the highest possible compliment to her, as woman and housekeeper, by taking her welcome (and fare) for granted.

Marion Harland's Complete Cook Book 1903

Woman accepted cooking as a chore, but man has made of it a recreation.

Emily Post, *Etiquette* 1922

A good cook is not necessarily a good woman with an even temper. Some allowance should be made for the artistic temperament. . . . Do not be unreasonable and suddenly announce at 7 o'clock that there will be three extra people for dinner. Cooks are only human beings and cannot work miracles.

X. Marcel Boulestin, *Simple French Cooking for English Homes* 1923

Some people make too much of a business of cooking. Properly managed, cooking is the simplest of work, but nowhere is an efficiency expert so needed as in the kitchen. There is nothing I hate more than to see a woman, hot, tired, and untidy from cooking a dinner I am supposed to eat. It takes all the pleasure out of the meal.

G. F. Scotson-Clark, *Eating Without Fears* 1924

To possess a cook who makes perfect soups is to possess a jewel of great price. A woman who cannot make soup should not be allowed to marry. . . . I often wonder why the judges who try the lamentable divorce cases of modern England do not inquire, when faced by the inevitable charges of mutual incompatibility, "What used you to give your husband for dinner?"

P. Morton Shand, *A Book of Food* 1928

Cooking I look upon as one of the real pleasures of life, and I always chafe a little when my wife assumes complete charge and I am edged out of the kitchen.

Lewis Mumford, in Marian Squire, *The Stag at Ease* 1938

"Who in hell," I said to myself, "wants to try to make pies like Mother makes, when it's so much simpler to let Mother make 'em in the first place?"

H. Arnow, *The Dollmaker* 1954

They say in Fife, that next to nae wife, the best thing is a gude wife.

Elizabeth Craig, *The Scottish Cookery Book* 1956

Naturally I like to cook, and it's a damned good thing that I do, because my wife went to Smith.

John Keats, in *The Artists' and Writers' Cookbook* 1961

In old China, in modest homes, the wife who cooked well was considered a pearl of great price. She was valued more for her culinary skill than for her beauty. Beauty fades, but a good cook improves with age. Her husband would never think of leaving her, since he couldn't bear the prospect of a future without her food.

Dr. Lee Su Jan, *The Fine Art of Chinese Cooking* 1962

I have always believed that among his unalienable rights, a man has a right to cook: especially Sunday breakfast when time is not of the essence. He should be able to cook the things he wants the way he wants them and when he wants them. And I propose that he do it alone. For there's nothing more disturbing to a man in the kitchen than a woman.

William C. Roux, *Fried Coffee and Jellied Bourbon* 1967

Women are like cheese strudels. When first baked, they are crisp and fresh on the outside, but the filling is unsettled and indigestible; in age, the crust may not be so lovely, but the filling comes at last into its own.

Robert Farrar Capon, *The Supper of the Lamb* 1969

Most of our grandmothers were no great shakes in the kitchen. They spent more time there than women do today, but what came out of their hard work was often no match for what a new bride can turn out today.

James Trager, *The Food Book* 1970

For a good dinner and a gentle wife, you can afford to wait.

Danish Proverb

Hospitality and Visitors

Not on the store of sprightly wine, nor plenty of delicious meats,
Though generous Nature did design to court us with perpetual
treats,—
'Tis not on these we for content depend, so much as on the shadow of
a Friend.

Menander, *Of Brotherly Love* ca. 300 B.C.

To me forever be that Guest unknown,
Who measuring my Expenses by his own,
Remarks the difference with a scornful leer,
And slights my Humble House and Homely Cheer.

Juvenal, *Eleventh Satire* A.D. 126

If there come any gesst, be circumspecte; see nothynge do wante.
Of necessary thynges be not skant, as breade & drynke. See there
be plentie.

F. Seager, *The Schoole of Vertue* 1557

Wife, make us a dinner, spare flesh neither corn;
Make wafers and cakes, for our sheep must be shorn.
At sheep-shearing neighbours none other thing crave
But good cheer and welcome, like neighbours to have.
Good fellow, good neighbour, that fellowly guest,
With heartile welcome should have of the best.
Three dishes well dressed, and welcome with all,
Both pleaseth thy friend and becometh thy hall.

Thomas Tusser, *Five Hundreth Pointes of Good Husbandrie* 1557

Sit down and feed, and welcome to our table.

William Shakespeare, *As You Like It* 1600

Those whose Purses cannot reach to the cost of rich Dishes . . . may
give, though upon a sudden Treatment, to their Kindred, Friends,

Allies and Aquaintance a handsome and relishing entertainment in all
seasons of the year, though at some distance from Towns and Villages.

Robert May, *The Accomplisht Cook* 1671

There are some Persons so excessive rude,
   that to your private Table they'll intrude.
In vain you fly, in vain pretend to fast,
   turn like a Fox, they'll catch you at the last.
You must, since Bars and Doors are no Defence,
   ev'n quit your House as in a Pestilence.
Be quick, nay, very quick, or he'll approach,
   and as you're scampering, stop you in your Coach.

William King, *The Art of Cookery* 1709

Now stir the fire, and close the shutters fast,
Let fall the curtains, wheel the sofa round,
And while the bubbling and loud-hissing urn
Throws up a steamy column, and the cups
That cheer, but not inebriate, wait on each,
So let us welcome peaceful evening in.

William Cowper, *The Task* 1785

More intent on the improvement of the understanding than the
gratification of the palate, the polished Athenian strove to delight his
guests not by the profusion of his dishes or multitude of his wines, but
by the discussion of useful and interesting topics of conversation.

Rev. Richard Warner, *Antiquitatis Culinariae* 1791

Everybody that have country seats are at them; and those that have
none visit others that have.

Arthur Young, *Travels in France during the Years 1787, '88 & '89* 1793

On the ridiculous vanity of those who wish to make an appearance
above their fortune: Nothing can be more ruinous to real comfort than

the too common custom of setting out a table with a parade and a profusion unsuited not only to the circumstances of the hosts, but to the number of guests; or more fatal to true hospitality, than the multiplicity of dishes which luxury has made fashionable at the tables of the great, the wealthy, and the ostentatious.

Dr. William Kitchiner, *The Cook's Oracle* 1817

Some persons suppose that they cannot preserve an air of hospitality without profusion: but they are egregiously mistaken; for, with a little management a table may be genteelly furnished, at an expense comparatively small, yet so as will give it a decided superiority over the lavish and even clumsy feasts provided by many hospitable and well-meaning people who, not knowing a medium between profusion and meanness, would despise perhaps that respectable kind of frugality which is here recommended.

Mrs. Ann Taylor, *Practical Hints to Young Females* 1822

In giving a dinner, the error is usually on the side of abundance.

Thomas Cooper, *Domestic Cookery* 1824

Dinner parties are very expensive and certainly fall very heavy on persons whose incomes are moderate; such persons, therefore, should not support a custom productive of unpleasant consequences.

Elizabeth Hammond, *Modern Domestic Cookery* 1825

With their plain dinner, and pleasant conversation, they pass half an hour and even more; sometimes sitting till 1 o'clock, especially if they have company. If the most illustrious visitors are present, they add nothing to the bread and potatoes, or whatever plain dishes they happen to have on the table, except perhaps some one kind of the best fruit of the season; and they never make any apologies.

William A. Alcott, *Ways of Living* 1837

Thrice happy days! In rural business passed;
Blest winter nights! when, as the genial fire
Cheers the wide hall, his cordial family
With soft domestic arts and hours beguile. . . .
Sometimes at eve, his neighbors lift the latch,
And bless unbid his festal roof;
While, o'er the light repast and sprightly cups,
They mix in social joy;
And through the maze of conversation
Trace whate'er amuses or improves the mind.

John Armstrong, *The Art of Preserving Health* 1838

When inviting company, do not tempt the palate by a great variety of unhealthful dainties.

Catherine E. Beecher, *A Treatise on Domestic Economy* 1845

You must always be prepared for friends who "drop in." A little attention to the side-board on such occasions frequently does more than a grand dinner.

One Who "Makes Ends Meet," *Economy for the Single & Married* 1845

No one need be ashamed of plain dinners if given with a hearty welcome.

Anonymous, *Table Observances* 1854

I had more visitors while I lived in the woods than at any other period of my life. But fewer came to see me on trivial business. In this respect, my company was winnowed by my mere distance from town. . . . I have had twenty-five or thirty souls, with their bodies, at once, under my roof. . . . If one guest came he sometimes partook of my frugal meal, and it was no interruption to conversation to be stirring a hasty-pudding, or watching the rising and maturing of a loaf of bread in the ashes, in the meanwhile. But if twenty came and sat in my house there was nothing said about dinner. We naturally practised abstinence, as if eating were a forsaken habit.

Henry David Thoreau, *Walden* 1854

Of all dinners, when it can be managed in any way, the impromptu
one is ranked as the most infallibly successful; the enjoyment therein
is proportioned to the absence of ceremony, and to the cordial feeling
each guest brings with him.

Charles Pierce, *The Household Manager* 1857

[Thoreau] declined invitations to dinner-parties, because there each
was in everyone's way, and he could not meet the individuals to any
purpose. "They make their pride," he said, "in making their dinner
cost much; I make my pride in making my dinner cost little." When
asked at table what dish he preferred, he answered, "The nearest."

Ralph Waldo Emerson, *Thoreau* 1862

The golden rule for giving dinners is, let all dinners be according to
the means of the givers. It is a great mistake for people of moderate
means to attempt to imitate the dinners of the rich. Also, the smaller
the dinner, the better will be the chance of its being well cooked.

John Timbs, *Lady Bountiful's Legacy* 1862

Our table was plentiful, but plain. If a friend came to take a meal with
us, our rule was to make no deviation from our usual fare. (Although it
invariably happens that if unexpected company comes in to a meal it is
on the days when you have no dessert provided, or a make-up, scrap
dinner.) On principle, we refrained from useless profusion. We could
not afford to make feasts or to give parties, and while we endeavoured
to "use hospitality without grudging" we also remembered that to live
beyond one's means is not consistent with reason or religion. In my
own visiting experience, I always found that a warm welcome and a
cordial spirit was a surer source of gratification to the guest than a
table loaded with costly viands.

Anonymous, *$600 a Year: A Wife's Effort at Low Living under High Prices* 1867

I have a well-set table on all occasions. I make no change for visitors,
whether believers or unbelievers. I intend never to be surprised by an

unreadiness to entertain at my table from one to half a dozen extra who may chance to come in. I have enough simple, healthful food ready to satisfy hunger and nourish the system. If any want more than this, they are at liberty to find it elsewhere.

Ellen G. White, *Life and Teachings* 1870

What to do with these brisk young men who break through all fences, and make themselves at home in every house?

Ralph Waldo Emerson, *Society and Solitude* 1870

A choice meal does not necessarily imply great expense, or great skill in preparation. The first requisite for a good dinner is good sense.

William Jones, *Take My Advice* 1872

The having too much, and setting dishes on the table merely for appearance, are practices arising out of prejudices, which, if once broken through, would be looked upon, and deservedly, as the height of vulgarity.

Henry Southgate, *Things a Lady Would Like to Know* 1874

When the barbarous practise of stuffing one's guests shall have been abolished, a social gathering will not necessarily imply hard work, and dyspepsia.

A. M. Diaz, *Papers Found in the School Master's Trunk* 1875

With regard to company—though it is a word I dislike excessively—there is much difference of opinion. Some people like to be made a fuss of. Such guests would consider themselves insulted at the menu I fear I should prepare for them, though I can assure them most earnestly they would feel much better next day after partaking of simple, perfectly prepared food than after dining on a mixture of badly-cooked unwholesome mixtures.

Lady Barker, *Houses and Housekeeping* 1876

The hospitality of a home should not have a superfluous magnificence and display which overawes and embarrasses the guest, making him feel ill at ease and self-conscious, while the hospitality itself becomes to the entertainer a burden too heavy to be borne. Our hospitality should be easy, brotherly, ready, and offered in that quiet simplicity which gives best opportunity for the steady conduct of our ordinary home-life.

Mrs. Julia McNair Wright, *The Complete Home* 1879

To revolutionize a whole house on the coming of a few visitors betrays not only poor taste, but an absolute lack of character. Let your friends come into your life; let them see you as you are, and not find you trying to be somebody else.

Emma Whitcomb Babcook, *Household Hints* 1881

The object of a good dinner-party is not to make a display of plate, china, flowers, or cookery, nor to gorge the party with the endless viands of a City feast, but to promote agreeable social intercourse and cheerful conversation, and to leave on the memory of those who have been invited to it the impression that they have passed a pleasant evening.

Mrs. Henry Reeve, *Cookery and Housekeeping* 1882

Two safe rules for entertaining are: Seldom apologize; never pretend. If you don't have dinner in three courses beside dessert every day, and you *know* Henrietta or Penelope doesn't either, why trouble yourself and the maid with changes of plates, and bringing in coffee in the small cups, and having out the finger-bowls that you use precisely a dozen times a year?

Mrs. S. D. Power, *Anna Maria's Housekeeping* 1884

Everybody who has ever lived in the country knows by experience what it is to have company descend upon them just a little before dinner-time, who have come to make a day of it. There is less of this informal visiting in the city than in the country because the time of city people is so taken up, and they have so many engagements that it is generally understood that visits are to be made only on invitation; and there is always a certain delicacy felt about going, even to the house of a friend, to dine unless specially bidden. But the limitations that hedge about city social intercourse are unheeded in the country, and the conventions are not so strictly regarded.

Sallie Joy White, *Housekeepers and Home-Makers* 1888

It is not every hostess who loves simplicity that dares to practise it.

Catherine Owen, *Choice Cookery* 1889

When a person visits you, remember he's your guest,
Receive him very kindly, and be sure he has the best.

Gelett Burgess, *Goops and How to Be Them* 1904

I hate guests who complain of the cooking and leave bits and pieces all over the place and cream-cheese sticking to the mirrors.

Colette, *Chéri* 1920

Here—in spite of snow, sleet, frost and biting winds—are the Thompsons.

Cartoon in *Punch* 1920

My father used to say, "Superior people never make long visits."

Marianne Moore, *Collected Poems* 1935

With plenty of house room, food and—if you like—homemade drink, one can entertain without much regard to cost. We often have one to a dozen house or dinner guests six days out of seven. On one occasion we provided for fifteen unexpected visitors at a Sunday evening supper.

Henry Tetlow, *We Farm for a Hobby and Make It Pay* 1938

After they have taken up farming, many a city man and his wife—and particularly his wife—have run the gamut of emotions through all the descending scale of delight, gratification, pleasure, surprise, perplexity, annoyance, disgust and exasperation (a full octave) to discover how popular they have become since moving to the country.

Not only do their intimate friends drop in unannounced on fine Sundays, but less and less intimate ones, even down to people who just happened to live around the block, arrive in auto loads and all expect to remain for dinner, perhaps supper also.

City people actually think that because farmers grow their own grain, hay, fruits, vegetables, and live stock, these things don't cost anything. They don't take into account the fact that if the farmer were to take or to ship these same products to market he could exchange them for cash, and that therefore he is giving away their money's worth, plus his wife's time, and whatever is added to them to prepare them for the table.

Unwelcome visitors, having learned of Jean's delicious meals, came in increasing numbers, so we discussed plans to check if not halt the procession. As you will probably have to solve the same problem, let me tell you the answer: for Sunday dinners have corned beef and cabbage, beef stew or hash.

M. G. Kains, *Five Acres and Independence* 1942

We learned to be chary of roads; they mean people, and commotion, and lack of peace.

Herbert Jacobs, *We Chose the Country* 1948

Solitude and Contentment

Better a dry morsel and quietness therewith, than a house full of feasting, with strife.

Anonymous, *Proverbs for Daily Living* undated

Oh! the blessings of privacy and leisure! The very thought and hope of it is a consolation, even in the middle of all the tumults and hazards that attend greatness. The Emperor Augustus prayed that he might live to retire, and deliver himself from public business. The highest felicity which this mighty prince had in prospect was the divesting himself of that illustrious state, which how glorious soever in show, had at the bottom of it only anxiety and care.

As long as we live in public, business breaks in upon us, as one billow drives on another, and there is no avoiding it with either modesty or quiet. It is a kind of whirlpool that sucks a man in, and he can never disengage himself. A man of business cannot in truth be said to live, and not one of a thousand understands how to do it. It is the greatest of all miseries to be perpetually employed upon other people's business; for to sleep, to eat, to drink at their hours, to walk their pace, and to love and hate as they do, is the vilest of servitudes.

Seneca, *Of a Happy Life* A.D. 54

Let us, I pray you, make our escape at length and spend in solitude what little time remains, taking every precaution that, while we seem to be bringing aid to the ship-wrecked, we be not ourselves overwhelmed by the waves or shattered against the rocks of human activities.

Francesco Petrarch, *De Vita Solitaria* 1356

Whoever loves the country, and lives in it upon his owne estate, whether hereditarie or purchased, and lends not his ears to any flatt'ring allurements perswading to ambition and greatnesse, but carefully avoids those dangerous precipices and quicksands, I shall not feare to affirme that such a liver is the wisest of men, for he, living upon his own, is no man's debtour, and is offensive to none but either a courtier or a citizen, and therefore is much more happy than if he had ingrost to himself all court favours, or had bin expert in the subtiltie and politicks of all forraign nations.

He fears no discontents to disturbe his peace, but lives well-pleased with what providence gives him, though never so little. He is free from all fretting cares, and is fed with no man's provision but his own. The crop of his land comes in certainly once a yeare; it is got with a good conscience, and is ever ready upon any necessity.

Don Antonio de Guevara, *The Praise & Happinesse of the Countrie-Life* 1539

Muse not, my friend, to finde me here,
Contented with this meane estate:
And seeme to doo with willing cheere,
That courtier doth so deadly hate.
From daintie Court to countrie fare,
Too daintie fed is diet strange:
From cities joy, to countrie care,
To skillesse folke is homelie change.

My friend, if cause doth wrest thee,
Ere follie hath much opprest thee:
Farre from acquaintance kest thee,
Where countrie may digest thee.
Let wood and water request thee,
In good corne soile to nest thee,
Where pasture and meade may brest thee,
And heathsom aire invest thee.
Though envie shall detest thee,
Let that no whit molest thee.
Thank God, that so hath blest thee,
And sit downe, Robin, and rest thee.

Thomas Tusser, *Five Hundreth Pointes of Good Husbandrie* 1557

O happy who thus liveth! Not caring much for gold;
With clothing which sufficeth to keep him from the cold,
Though poor and plain his diet, yet merry 'tis, and quiet.

Elizabethan Song Book ca. 1588

A little lowly hermitage it was
Downe in a dale, hard by a forest's side,
Far from resort of people that did pass
In traveill to and froe.

Edmund Spenser, The Fairie Queene 1590

What I eat in my own corner without compliments or ceremonies, though it were nothing but bread and an onion, relishes better than turkey at other folk's tables, where I am forced to eat leisurely, drink little, wipe my mouth often, and can neither sneeze nor cough when I have a mind.

Miguel de Cervantes, Don Quixote 1605

Doe you yet marvaile how I can delight my selfe with this so honest and profitable a quietnes, then which in the judgement of the holiest and wisest men, there is nothing more honest nor better, neither is there beside any trade of life more meet for a Gentleman, nor travaile more acceptable to God, than is the tilling of the ground.

Barnaby Googe, The Whole Art and Trade of Husbandry 1614

If Eden be on earth at all,
'Tis that which we the country call.

Henry Vaughan, Poems 1646

Blest be the man (and blest is he) whom e'er
(Plac'd far out of the roads of hope or fear)
A little field, a little garden feeds;
The field gives all that frugal nature needs,
The wealthy garden liberally bestows
All she can ask, when she luxuriant grows.
The specious inconveniences that wait
Upon a life of business, and of state,
He sees (nor does the sight disturb his rest)
By fools desired, by wicked men possest.

Abraham Cowley, Essays in Verse & Prose 1668

Here the Nightingale is constrain'd to stay without any other cage than that of the native pleasures of the place; and here the Sun looks from morning to night with a pleasing countenance upon the off-springs of his own beams, neither clouded with smoak, nor intercepted by angles of falling houses. . . . Here the levelling though aspiring trees lay their heads together, to protect such as seek shelter under their well-cloath'd branches: and the Crystal streams run slowly and turn many windings, as if by that and their quiet murmurings they would express an unwillingness to leave so pleasant a field.

Sir George Mackenzie, *A Moral Essay,*
Preferring Solitude to Public Employment 1685

A safe retreat, a gentle solitude,
Unvexed with noise, and undisturbed with fears. . . .
From purling streams and savage fruits,
Have wholesome beverage, and bloodless feasts.

John Dryden, *Don Sebastian* 1689

Well, I have thought on't, and I find this busy world is nonsense all;
I here despair to please my mind, her sweetest honey is so mixt with gall.
Come then, I'll try how 'tis to be alone,
Live to myself a while, and be my own.

John Morris, *The Retirement* 1700

Oh, knew he but his happiness, of men
The happiest he! who far from public rage,
Deep in the vale, with a choice few retir'd,
Drinks the pure pleasures of the Rural Life.

James Thomson, *The Seasons* 1730

He who has fewest wants, and is most able to live within himself, is not only the happiest, but the richest man; and if he does not abound in what the world calls Wealth, he does in Independency.

Anonymous, *The Way to Be Rich and Respectable,*
addressed to Men of Small Fortune 1780

Happy man, dids't thou but know the extent of thy good fortune! . . .
This man devoid of society learns more than ever to center every idea
within that of his own welfare. To him all that appears good, just,
equitable has a necessary relation to himself and family. He has been
so long alone that he has almost forgot the rest of mankind except it is
when he carries his crops on the snow to some distant market.

> Michel Guillaume Crèvecouer, *Letters from an American Farmer* 1782

Had I the choice of sublunary good,
What could I wish, that I possess not here?
Health, leisure, means t'improve it, friendship, peace,
And constant occupation without care.
Oh! friendly to the best pursuits of man,
Friendly to thought, to virtue, and to peace,
Domestic life in rural pleasures passed!

> William Cowper, *The Task* 1785

A beechen bowl, a maple dish, my furniture should be:
Tired of the world and all its industry.

> William Wordsworth, *The Recluse* 1800

I learned this, at least, by my experiment, that if one advances
confidently in the direction of his dreams, and endeavors to live the
life which he has imagined, he will meet with a success unexpected in
common hours. He will put some things behind, will pass an invisible
boundary; new, universal, and more liberal laws will begin to establish
themselves around and within him; or the old laws be expanded, and
interpreted in his favor in a more liberal sense, and he will live with
the license of a higher order of beings. In proportion as he simplifies
his life, the laws of the universe will appear less complex, and solitude
will not be solitude, nor poverty poverty, nor weakness weakness. If
you have built castles in the air, your work need not be lost, that is
what they should be. Now put foundations under them.

> Henry David Thoreau, *Walden* 1854

No, I am a stranger in your towns. I am not at home at French's, or Lovejoy's, or Savery's. I can winter more to my mind amid the shrub oaks. I have made arrangements to stay with them.

Henry David Thoreau, *Journal* December 1, 1856

There is a class of men who gravitate to the country by a pure necessity of their nature; who have such ineradicable love for springing grass, and fields and woods, as to draw them irresistibly into companionship. Such men feel the confinement of a city like a prison. They are restive under its restraint.

D. G. Mitchell, *My Farm of Edgewood* 1863

I sought the country absolute, a cottage or a little farm remote from towns and out of sight of railways; villages so tiny that maps refuse to name them.

W. J. Dawson, *The Quest of the Simple Life* 1907

Truly, man made the city, and after he became sufficiently civilized, not afraid of solitude, and knew on what terms to live with nature, God promoted him to life in the country.

John Burroughs, *Songs and Seasons* 1914

No meal is as good as when you have your feet under your own table.

Scott Nearing, an opinion 1970

The Evening of Life

I come now to discourse of the pleasures which accompany the labours of the husbandman, and with which I myself am delighted beyond expression. They are pleasures which meet with no obstruction even from old age, and seem to approach nearest to those of true wisdom.

Cicero, *De Senectute* 45 B.C.

This is what I prayed for: a piece of land not so very large, where there is a garden, and near the house an ever-flowing spring of water, and above these a bit of woodland.

Horace, *Satires* 30 B.C.

That retreat is not worth the while which does not afford a man greater and nobler work than business. There is no slavish attendance upon great offices; no canvassing for places, no making of parties; no disappointments in my pretension to this charge, to that regiment, or to such or such a title; no envy of any man's favour or fortune; but a calm enjoyment of the general bounties of Providence, in company with a good Conscience.

Seneca, *Of a Happy Life* A.D. 54

Therefore the counseylles of auncyent & whyte heered men in whom olde age hath engendred wysdome hath ben gretely preysed of yonger men & shewe unto the reders & heerers by the ensamples of thynges passed, what thyng is to be desyred & what is to be eschewed.

Dan Ranulph Higden, Monke of Chester, *Polycronycon* 1527

Now pause with yourselfe, and view the end of all your Labours . . . unspeakable Pleasure and infinite Commodity.

William Lawson, *A New Orchard and Garden* 1648

I never had any other desire so strong, as so like to covetousness as that one, which I have had always, that I might bee master at last, of a small Hous and a larg Garden, with very moderate conveniences joyned to them, and there dedicat the remainder of my life, onely to the culture of them, and study of Nature. And there, with no design beyond my wall, whole and entire to lye, in no unactive Eas, and no unglorious Poverty.

Abraham Cowley, *The Garden* 1666

This only grant me, that my means may lie
Too low for envy, for contempt too high.
Some honour I would have,
Not from great deeds, but good alone.
The unknown are better than ill known.
Rumour can ope the grave;
Acquaintance I would have, but when 't depends
Not on the number, but the choice of friends.

Books should, not business, entertain the light,
And sleep, as undisturb'd as death, the night.
My house a cottage, more
Than palace, and should fitting be
For all my use, no luxury.
My garden painted o'er
With Nature's hand, not Art's; and pleasures yield
Horace might envy in his Sabine field.

Thus would I double my life's fading space,
For he that runs it well, twice runs the race.
And in this true delight,
These unbought sports, this happy state,
I would not fear nor wish my fate,
But boldly say each night,
Tomorrow let my sun his beams display,
Or in clouds hide them; I have liv'd today.

Abraham Cowley, *Essays in Verse & Prose* 1668

The ancient and best magistrates of Rome allow'd but the ninth day for the city and publick business; the rest for the country and the sallet garden. There were then fewer causes indeed at the bar, but never greater justice, nor better judges and advocates.

John Evelyn, *Acetaria* 1699

The Author blesseth God for his Retirement, and kisses that Gentle Hand which led him into it: For tho' it should prove Barren to the World, it can never do so to him. . . . And 'till we are perswaded to stop, and step a little Aside, out of the Noisy Crowd and Incumbering Hurry of the World, and calmly take a Prospect of Things, it will be impossible we should be able to make a right Judgment of our Selves, or know our own Misery. But after we have made the just Reckonings which Retirement will help us to, we shall begin to think the World in great Measure Mad, and that we have been in a Sort of Bedlam all this While.

William Penn, *Some Fruits of Solitude* 1726

As long as the World lasts, the Pleasures and Entertainments which Gardening and Agriculture afford, will be the pursuit of wise Men who, whilst they find & relish Retirement, will also find the Pleasure of enquiring into the Powers of Nature, whose Returns are abundant Recompences for their most laborious Searches. And happy surely they who find Satisfaction in those so innocent Pleasures, instead of disturbing the World or their Neighbours, when they cannot be quiet themselves, tho' no body hurts them.

The Evening of Life is thus, to be sure, most wisely and agreeably spent. When the Decline of Nature tends to pevishness and a froward Weakness, and we cannot so firmly bear the Frowns of Fortune, the Ingratitude of a Friend, the Malice and Treachery of an Enemy; then to step aside, as it were, out of the World a little before our Time, and give such a decent Turn to our Thoughts as may hide the Weaknesses of human Nature, and at the same Time recreate our Minds with innocent and advantageous Pleasures, hath always been and must always be, accounted Wisdon.

It must be owned, indeed, that the Town hath its Pleasures as well as the Countrey. But how alluring soever the Pleasures of the Town may seem to us, whilst Health and Strength and the Gaities of Youth last, Envy, Malice and Double-dealing do so frequent the most busy Parts of the World, which tend to mar all those Delights, we shall be inclined to declare in Favour of the innocent Simplicity of a Countrey-life.

John Laurence, *A New System of Agriculture* 1726

He certainly is worthy great Praise and Honour, who, possessing a large and barren Demesne, constrains it, by his Industry and Labour, to produce extraordinary Plenty, not only to his own Profit, but that of the Public also.

Sir Richard Weston, *Legacy to His Sons* 1759

Our life is a busy round of a great variety of occupations, all tending to health and chearfulness. We rise every day with the sun, and in the cool of morning, employ ourselves in business which requires some strength. The garden takes up much of our time. In the afternoon we read and work. In the evening I take to my tools and labour again, either hoeing, digging, chopping wood against winter, or any work of the season that is necessary. Such generally is the round of the day. . . . Our happy little farm yields us a constant amusement of a most rational and agreeable kind.

Arthur Young, *The Adventures of Emmera* 1767

Persons with circumscribed fortunes, or whose family encreases upon them, would do well to retrench their expences in time; or retire from towns, and lay out their money with economy. The occupier of a middling farm enjoys all the necessaries and conveniences of life, and many of its superfluities. Where shall we meet with better health, than where temperance and exercise enliven the mind, invigorate the body, and keep a constant flow of spirits? A new mode of living may at first be a little awkward; but the retirement of a year or two will produce such heart-felt satisfaction as will convince the person retiring, it was the best step he ever took in his life.

Anonymous, *The Way to Be Rich and Respectable,*
addressed to Men of Small Fortune 1780

The tide of life, swift always in its course,
May run in cities with a brisker force,
But no where with a current so serene
Or half so clear as in the rural scene.

Hackney'd in business, wearied at that oar
Which thousands once fast chain'd to, quit no more,
But which when life at ebb runs weak and low,
All wish, or seem to wish they could forego.

The statesman, lawyer, merchant, man of trade,
Pants for the refuge of some rural shade,
Where all his long anxieties forgot
Amid the farms of a sequester'd spot . . .
Improve the remnant of his wasted span,
And having liv'd a trifler, die a man.

To them the deep recess of dusky groves
Or forest, where the deer securely roves,
The fall of water, and the song of birds,
And hills that echo to the distant herds,
Are luxuries excelling all the glare
The world can boast, and her chief favorites share.

William Cowper, *Retirement* 1782

Thanking you for your felicitations on my present quiet. The difference of my present and past situation is such as to leave me nothing to regret, but that my retirement has been postponed four years too long. The principles on which I calculated the value of life, are entirely in favor of my present course. I return to farming with an ardor which I scarcely knew in my youth, and which has got the better entirely of my love of study. Instead of writing ten or twelve letters a day, which I have been in the habit of doing as a thing in course, I put off answering my letters now, farmer-like, till a rainy day, and then find them sometimes postponed by other necessary occupations.

Thomas Jefferson, *Letter to George Washington* April 25, 1794

Have you become a farmer? Is it not pleasanter than to be shut up within four walls and delving eternally with the pen? . . . I have proscribed newspapers. . . . My next reformation will be to allow neither pen, ink nor paper to be kept on the farm. When I have accomplished this, I shall be in a fair way of indemnifying myself for the drudgery in which I have passed my life. If you are half as much delighted with the farm as I am, you bless your stars at your riddance from public cares.

Thomas Jefferson, *Letter to Henry Knox* 1795

Rural scenery is so congenial to the human mind, that there are few persons who do not indulge the hope of retiring at some period into the country. Its peculiar and gentle pleasures are suited to all ages and every rank of life, and afford not less gratification to the general observer, than to the philosopher, the poet, or the painter.

Those who enjoy a country residence have an opportunity of adding to the charms of rural scenery, the pleasures resulting from agriculture and gardening. These recreations are almost equally congenial with the human mind; and the pleasure that attends their pursuit is still farther recommended by their utility in life and their influence on society.

Such is the superiority of rural occupations and pleasures, that commerce, large societies, or crowded cities, may be justly reckoned unnatural. Indeed, the very purpose for which we engage in commerce is, that we may one day be enabled to retire to the country, where alone we picture to ourselves days of solid satisfaction and undisturbed happiness. It is evident that such sentiments are natural to the human mind.

J. C. Loudon, *A Treatise on Forming,*
Improving & Managing Country Residences 1806

Good! A remedy without physician, gold or sorcery:
Away forthwith, and to the fields repair,
Begin to delve, to cultivate the ground,
Thy senses and thyself confine
Within the very narrowest round.

Support thyself, upon the simplest fare.
Live like a very brute the brutes among.
Neither esteem it robbery
The acre thou dost reap, thyself to dung.
This is the best method, credit me,
Again at eighty, to grow hale and young.

Goethe, *Faust* 1808

I am retired to Monticello where I enjoy a repose to which I have been long a stranger. My mornings are devoted to correspondence. From breakfast to dinner, I am in my shops, my garden, or on horseback among my farms; from dinner to dark, I give to society and recreation with my neighbors and my friends; and from candle-light to early bedtime, I read. My health is perfect, and my strength considerably reinforced by the activity of the course I pursue; perhaps it is as great as usually falls to the lot of near 67 years of age. I talk of plows and harrows, of seeding and harvesting with my neighbors, and of politics too, if they choose, with as little reserve as the rest of my fellow citizens, and feel, at length, the blessing of being free to say and do what I please, without being responsible to any mortal.

Thomas Jefferson, *Letter to Thaddeus Kosciusko* February 26, 1810

Such is the field of delightful action lying before me, that I am ready to regret the years wasted in the support of taxes and pauperism, and to grieve that I am growing old now, that a really useful career seems just beginning. I am happier, much happier, in my prospects. I feel that I am doing well for my family: and the Privations I anticipated seem to vanish before us.

Morris Birbeck, *Letters from Illinois* 1818

Many of our best citizens, who were distinguished in the field and in the cabinet, are now to be found on their farms, devoting their time and attention to the occupations of husbandry, as the surest means of gaining an honorable subsistence and of doing good to their country, by thus encouraging and patronizing this first of arts.

Agricola, *A Series of Essays on Agriculture and Rural Affairs* 1819

My farm, my family, my books and my building, give me much more pleasure than any public office would, and, especially, one which would keep me constantly far from them.

Thomas Jefferson, *Writings* 1820

May all those who are in possession of land, and are disposed to labour for their subsistence, have all those comforts and necessities of life which I am now in the full enjoyment of; indeed, I have no doubt as to the success of all parties, provided they have made up their minds to live, as I do, upon the produce of their land.

Besides the greatest of all benefits that I have derived in restoring a sickly constitution to perfect health, I felt delighted at the thought of being independent of the harassing cares of business. Of all the feelings which we possess, none is dearer than good conscience; and this no man who earns his living by the favour of the public, can be said to enjoy in an equal degree with the husbandman. In trade, there is a great jealousy and competition existing, and a submission to the public, which is galling to the spirits. But since I have given my attention to the cultivation of the soil, I find I have no competition to fear, have nothing to apprehend from the success of my neighbour, and owe no thanks for the purchase of my commodities. Possessing on my land all the necessaries of life, I am under no anxiety regarding my daily subsistence.

John Sillett, *A New Practical System of Fork & Spade Husbandry* 1850

Many who have not been brought up as farmers are looking for something which, with less mental toil and anxiety, will provide a maintenance for a growing family, and afford a refuge for advancing age—some safe and quiet harbor, sheltered from the constantly re-curring monetary and political convulsions which in this country so suddenly reduce men to poverty.

The reader must not take it for granted that in going into the country we escaped all the annoyances of domestic life peculiar to the city, or that we fell heir to no new ones, such as we had never before experienced. He must remember that this is a world of compensations, and that nowhere will he be likely to find either an unmixed good or an unmixed bad. Such was exactly our experience. But on summing up the two, the balance was decidedly in our favor.

Isaac Phillips Roberts, *Ten Acres Enough* 1864

Man, confined to the city by dire necessity of money-making, recognizing the country as the natural sphere of his existence, dreams of a neat, quiet, retired country place. Visions of the accomplished fact engrossed my mind, although by a strange fatality my education in country matters had been woefully neglected, for I could hardly distinguish tomato vines from egg-plants, and had not the remotest notion of modes or seasons of planting. But now there was a possibility that these imaginings might be realized.

Robert B. Roosevelt, *Five Acres Too Much* 1869

I have been seeking through all the valleys to acquire some isolated pasturage which will yet be easily accessible, moderately clement in temperature, pleasantly situated, watered by a stream, and within sound of a torrent or the waves of a lake. I have no wish for a pretentious domain. I prefer to select a convenient site and then build after my own fashion, with the view of locating myself for a time, or perhaps for always. An obscure valley would be for me the sole habitable earth.

E. P. de Senancour, *Obermann* 1903

Are these things within reach of the city-bred man who has sufficient means to invest in a medium-sized country place who wishes to make it pay? Most assuredly so, provided such a one has a real love for country life, a mind intelligent enough to grasp the principles on which success depends, and—added to these—the will to read, to work and to learn from the larger experience of others.

Edward K. Parkinson, *The Practical Country Gentleman* 1911

There was no going back now. I had thrown up my post and was rapidly sinking my little capital on the great venture in the open country. By some means I should have to wrest a living from the soil for myself, my wife and my child. There was no nest-egg to fall back upon, no private income to butter my bread. I had gotten down to the bed-rock of existence. Now I should feel something of the exhilaration of contending with Nature, of winning bread from the bare earth, and know the joy of creating something with my own hands and completing that which I had fashioned.

It is in the lack of creative joy that is to be found the insidious germ of the soul-deadening, manhood-destroying effects of city life, where the worker is only an unrecognized cog in a huge industrial machine.

I have never regretted the step I took. Among the multitudinous siren notes of city life there is not one to lure me back again. Fortunately, I have found sustenance in tilling the soil and am never in want of a fortifying dinner, for at hand are milk, honey, fruit and vegetables.

F. E. Green, *A Few Acres and a Cottage* 1911

Never was the back-to-the-land cry more prominent than today; never was it more serious. Other back-to-the-land cries have been but flashes in the pan, and for that very reason failed to materialise. One is now tempted to ask if the present revival will mature, and to study the type of men who are the participants. Our first thoughts fly towards the soldiers, hundreds of thousands of whom between 1914 and 1918 have had but one earnest desire—to return home and claim that "little place in the sun." A postal ballot showed that nearly a million men in our fighting forces wished to settle on the land. The thoughts of Arcadia must have stood many tens of thousands of our warriors in good stead in the darkest and coldest hours on the battlefield.

The fever has also made strong headway in the ranks of those civilians who have capital and who want to settle down on the land. Many of them, too old or rejected for the army, have caught the land craze as the result of their small war-efforts of increasing the nation's food supply and of feeding their families.

W. Powell-Owen, *A Living from the Land* 1919

If we had ample means and could choose any kind of life we wished, we would choose what we have chosen. And when I say we, I mean we. There are many differences between a man's viewpoint and a woman's, even though they may live side by side in the same house year in and year out. But there must be a profound unshaken unity underneath the difference if they are to make a success of such a life as we have lived, because the things that must be passed by are things that one or the other might consider indispensable. As for children, I cannot help but think that they gain far more than they lose, in happiness and experience. By and large, it is the best life for children. And later, they must make their own choice.

Gove Hambidge, *Enchanted Acre: Adventures in Backyard Farming* 1935

When humanity gets tired enough of being hounded from pillar to post, when the powerful have sufficiently persecuted the weak and the envious weak have sufficiently obstructed the strong, perhaps our way of life will come to seem the true one, the good one; and people everywhere will awake in astonishment at having for so long neglected its simple wisdom.

Louise Dickinson Rich, *My Neck of the Woods* 1950

Index

Abel, Mary Hinman, 40
Adamson, Helen Lyon, 41
Agricola, 169
Alcott, Amos Bronson, 66
Alcott, William A., 19, 20, 38, 93, 123–24, 133, 145
Allen, R. L., 66, 82
Andrews, Julia C., 134
Armstrong, John, 19, 28, 146
Arnow, H., 138

Babcook, Emma Whitcomb, 149
Bacon, Sir Francis, 55, 63
Baldwin, Faith, 59
Barker, Lady, 40, 84, 148
Barnum, H. L., 122
Bates, Ely, 6–7
Beecher, Catherine E., 84, 125, 135, 146
Beeton, Isabella, 135
Beeton, S. O., 67
Birbeck, Morris, 169
Blake, Rev. John L., 93, 134
Bonta, Edwin, 77–78
Boorde, Andrewe, 4, 15, 71–72, 90
Booth, E. T., 31
Bordley, John B., 19
Boulestine, X. Marcel, 137
Bradley, R., 120–21
Breton, Nicholas, 36, 120
Brissot de Warville, J. P., 110
Brown, Susan Anna, 40
Brownell, Baker, 104
Burgess, Gelett, 150
Burke, Edmund, 28

Burns, Robert, 110
Burroughs, John, 76–77, 160
Byrd, William, 6

Capon, Robert Farrar, 127, 139
Carew, Richard, 55
Carpenter, Edward, 30, 104
Cato the Censor, 71, 99
Cervantes, Miguel de, 157
Chaucer, Geoffrey, 55, 131
Chesterfield, Earl of, 90
Cheyne, Dr. George, 18
Chiang Yea, 11–12
Child, Mrs. Lydia Maria, 39
Churchill, Charles, 110
Cicero, 3, 63, 99, 163
Clare, John, 111
Clarke, Elizabeth, 60, 127
Cobbett, William, 38, 101, 111
Coffin, Robert P. Tristram, 51
Coleridge, Samuel Taylor, 56
Coles, William, 63
Colette, 150
Coomaraswamy, Ananda K., 115
Cooper, Thomas, 81, 145
Cooper, William, 92, 101
Copley, Esther, 38, 82, 123
Cornaro, Louis, 19
Cowley, Abraham, 5, 16–17, 64, 102, 103, 132, 157, 163–64
Cowper, William, 144, 159, 167
Craig, Elizabeth, 138
Craik, Dinah Mulock, 67
Crèvecoeur, Michel Guillaume, 27, 159

Damon, Bertha, 41
Davidson, Bruce, 87
Dawson, W. J., 10–11, 30, 113, 160
Deane, Samuel, 56, 65
Democritus, 45
Diaz, A. M., 48, 84, 136, 148
Dick, Stewart, 77
Donaldson, James, 26, 90
Dryden, John, 158

Eliot, Jared, 55, 64, 91, 100
Elyot, Sir Thomas, 16
Emerson, Ralph Waldo, 7–8, 29, 39,
    58, 76, 85, 102, 112, 147, 148
Evelyn, John, 5, 17, 26, 36, 64,
    164–65

Fessenden, Thomas G., 28, 65, 66,
    101
Franklin, Benjamin, 37
Fuller, Thomas, 41

Ghesel, John, 16
Gilman, Charlotte, 93
Gilpin, William, 81
Goethe, Johann Wolfgang von, 169
Goldsmith, Oliver, 46
Goodfellow, Mrs., 135
Googe, Barnaby, 4–5, 73, 157
Gordon, Martha H., 136
Gourgas, J. M., 46, 93
Gray, Thomas, 110
Green, E. F., 30, 171–72
Guevara, Don Antonio de, 4, 15,
    100, 155–56

Haggard, H. Rider, 58, 67, 86
Hale, Sarah Josepha, 47, 82, 124,
    133
Hall, Bolton, 10

Hambidge, Gove, 173
Hammond, Elizabeth, 145
Harland, Marion, 49, 125, 137
Harrison, Mary, 113, 126
Helme, John, 16
Hemstreet, William, 9–10
Henderson, George, 67
Hesiod, 71
Higden, Dan Randolph, 163
Higginson, Francis, 36, 81
Holinshed, Raphael, 72, 119
Horace, 4, 15, 71, 163
Howard, Henry, 4
Howitt, William, 57
Huxley, Julian, 95

Ignatus, 38

Jackson, Helen Hunt, 58
Jacobs, Herbert, 151
Jefferson, Thomas, 7, 74, 101, 167,
    168, 169, 170
Jones, William, 148
Juvenal, 143

Kains, M. G., 151
Keats, John, 138
King, William, 144
Kipling, Rudyard, 30, 86
Kitchiner, Dr. William, 19, 111,
    121, 144–45
Krutch, Joseph Wood, 115

Lacordaire, Henri, 8
Lathrop, Leonard E., 7, 92
Laurence, John, 6, 166
Lawson, William, 26, 63, 163
Lee, Mrs. N. K. M., 122
Lee Su Jan, Dr., 138
Le Jeune, Paul, 25

Leland, E. H., 76
Lemery, Dr. M. L., 18
Lessius, L., 37
Lin Yutang, 21–22, 114
Loudon, J. C., 7, 81, 93, 95, 101,
   102, 111, 168
Lowie, Robert H., 86
Lyman, J. B. and L. E., 125

McCarrison, Sir Robert, 22
McDougall, Francis Harriet, 81
Mackenzie, Sir George, 26, 158
Markham, Gervase, 25, 46, 73,
   119–20
May, Robert, 144
Mayerne, Sir Thomas, 131
Melville, Herman, 59
Menander, 143
Miller, Philip, 27
Milton, John, 131
Mitchell, D. G., 75, 94–95, 160
Moffett, Thomas, 16
Moore, Marianne, 150
Morris, John, 158
Morse, Edmund S., 9
Mortimer, J., 73
Mottram, V. H., 21
Mumford, Lewis, 138
Munthe, Axel, 105

Nearing, Scott, 160

Owen, Catherine, 85, 150

Packard, Clarissa, 123
Pallis, Marco, 115
Parker, Mrs. William, 121–22
Parkinson, Edward K., 171
Parley, Peter, 56–57
Payne, A. G., 95

Penn William, 18, 27, 36–37, 165
Peters, Frazier, 78
Petrarch, Francesco, 99, 155
Philp, R. K., 112
Pickering, James, 28
Pierce, Charles, 134, 147
Pinkham, T. J., 94, 112
Post, Emily, 137
Powell-Owen, W., 172
Power, Mrs. S. D., 49–50, 149

Quarles, Francis, 109–10

Randolph, John, 101
Read, Herbert, 78
Reed, William, 84–85, 113
Reeve, Mrs. Henry, 149
Rich, Louise Dickenson, 173
Richards, Ella H., 126
Richardson, Richard, 58
Roberts, Isaac Phillips, 29, 58, 66,
   171
Robinson, Solon, 20–21, 83
Roosevelt, Robert B., 171
Rose, John, 64
Roux, William C., 138
Rumford, Count, 38
Rundell, Mary Eliza, 121, 132
Ruskin, John, 29, 103

Scotson-Clark, G. F., 137
Scott, Mrs. M. L., 124
Seager, F., 143
Secundus, D. Humbergius, 47
Senancour, E. P. de, 113, 171
Seneca, 35, 109, 155, 163
Shakespeare, William, 55, 109, 143
Shand, P. Morton, 137
Sharp, Benjamin, 8
Shay, Frank, 87

Shenstone, William, 9
Sherwood, M. E. W., 136
Sigourney, Mrs. L. H., 123
Sillett, John, 170
Smith, F. D., 30
Smith, Captaine John, 73
Smith, Prudence, 122, 132
Smith, W. L., 114
Southgate, Henry, 148
Soyer, Alexis, 133
Spenser, Edmund, 157
Stevenson, Robert Louis, 103
Street, A. G., 31, 59
Strickland, Samuel, 74, 82–83
Swift, Jonathan, 5
Swissholm, Jane G., 124

Talbot, E. A., 111
Tarbell, Ida, M., 126
Taylor, Mrs. Ann, 145
Tetlow, Henry, 11, 50–51, 86–87, 95, 104, 150
Thomson, James, 158
Thoreau, Henry David, 9, 20, 29, 57, 74–75, 83, 93, 94, 112, 133, 146, 159, 160
Thudicum, J. L. W., 85–86
Timbs, John, 147
Toynbee, Philip, 96
Trager, James, 139
Traill, C. P., 57, 135
Tryon, Thomas, 5, 17, 18, 26, 36, 55
Tusser, Thomas, 16, 25, 35, 45, 63, 72, 90, 119, 131, 143, 156

Twain, Mark, 77

Vaughan, Beatrice, 41
Vaughan, Henry, 157
Vaughan, William, 16, 81
Virgil, 3–4, 25

Wagner, Charles, 104
Wahl, Dr. Carl C., 22
Walker, Francis A., 103–04
Warner, Charles Dudley, 66
Warner, Rev. Richard, 144
Warren, Mrs. Eliza, 39, 125
Washington, George, 6
Weaver, Richard, 78
Weston, Sir Richard, 166
White, Ellen G., 20, 21, 48, 148
White, Sallie Joy, 150
Whitman, Walt, 75, 83
Whittier, John Greenleaf, 84
Wiggin, Kate Douglas, 126
Wilcox, B., 30
Wooley, Hannah, 120
Wordsworth, William, 159
Wright, Alexander, 127
Wright, Frank Lloyd, 104, 115
Wright, Mrs. Julia McNair, 149
Wright, Richardson, 11, 59

Xenophon, 63

Young, Arthur, 28, 91, 144, 166

CHELSEA GREEN

Sustainable living has many facets. Chelsea Green's celebration of the sustainable arts has led us to publish trend-setting books about organic gardening, solar electricity and renewable energy, innovative building techniques, regenerative forestry, local and bioregional democracy, and whole foods. The company's published works, while intensely practical, are also entertaining and inspirational, demostrating that an ecological approach to life is consistent with producing beautiful, eloquent, and useful books, videos, and audio cassettes.

For more information about Chelsea Green, or to request a free catalog, call toll-free (800) 639-4099, or write to us at P.O. Box 428, White River Junction, Vermont 05001. Visit our Web site at www.chelseagreen.com. Chelsea Green's titles include:

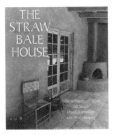
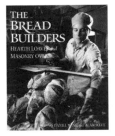

The Straw Bale House
The Independent Home:
    Living Well with Power from
    the Sun, Wind,
    and Water
Independent Builder:
    Designing & Building a
    House Your Own Way
The Rammed Earth House
The Passive Solar House
The Sauna
Wind Power for Home &
    Business
The Solar Living Sourcebook
A Shelter Sketchbook
Mortgage-Free!
Hammer. Nail. Wood.

The Bread Builders:
    Hearth Loaves and
    Masonry Ovens
Whole Foods Companion
The Apple Grower
The Flower Farmer
Passport to Gardening:
    A Sourcebook for the
    21st-Century
The New Organic Grower
Four-Season Harvest
Solar Gardening
Straight-Ahead Organic
The Contrary Farmer
The Contrary Farmer's
    Invitation to Gardening
Forest Gardening

Loving and Leaving the
    Good Life
Scott Nearing: The Making
    of a Homesteader
Gaviotas: A Village to
    Reinvent the World
Who Owns the Sun?
Global Spin:
    The Corporate Assault
    on Environmentalism
Hemp Horizons
A Patch of Eden
A Place in the Sun
Renewables Are Ready
Beyond the Limits
The Man Who Planted Trees
The Northern Forest